Ralph Fitch,

Elizabethan in the Indies

Great Travellers

General Editor: George Woodcock

Alexander Mackenzie and the North West
Roy Daniells

Australia's Last Explorer: Ernest Giles
Geoffrey Dutton

Bokhara Burnes
James Lunt

Henry Walter Bates, Naturalist of the Amazon
George Woodcock

Into Tibet the Early British Explorers
George Woodcock

Magellan of the Pacific
Edouard Roditi

Papal Envoys to the Great Khans
I. de Rachewitz

Thomas Gage in Spanish America
Norman Newton

RALPH FITCH
ELIZABETHAN IN THE INDIES

by
Michael Edwardes

With Fitch our Eldred next, deserv'dly placed is,
Both travelling to see the Syrian Tripolis.
The first of which (in this whose noble spirit was shown)
To view those parts, to us that were the most unknown,
On thence to Ormus set, Goa, Cambaya, then,
To vast Zelabdim, thence to Echebar, again
Crossed Ganges' mighty stream, and his large banks did view,
To Bacola went on, to Bengola, Pegu;
And for Mallaccan then, Zeiten, and Cochin cast
Measuring with many a step, the great East-Indian waste.

MICHAEL DRAYTON *Poly-Olbion* (1612)

FABER AND FABER
3 Queen Square
London

First published in 1972
by Faber and Faber Limited
3 Queen Square London WC1
Printed in Great Britain by
Butler & Tanner Ltd, Frome and London

ISBN 0 571 10133 X

Preface

'IN THE yeere of our Lord 1583, I Ralph Fitch of London marchant being desirous to see the countreys of the East India . . . did ship my selfe in a ship of London called the Tyger . . .'

So begins the account of a pioneer journey made by one of the first Englishmen to set foot in India and travel through the dominions of the Great Mogul, and the very first to penetrate as far as Burma, Thailand and Malaya. The narrative first appeared in print in that vast compendium of contemporary geographical knowledge, Richard Hakluyt's *Principal Navigations Voyages Traffiques and Discoveries of the English Nation*, in 1599.

Hakluyt whets the imagination by prefacing Fitch's story with a foretaste of what is to come. Master Fitch's journey had taken him 'by the way of Tripolis in Syria, to Ormus, and so to Goa in the East India, to Cambaia, and all the kingdoms of Zelabdim Echebar the great Mogor, to the mighty river Ganges, and downe to Bengala, to Bacola, and Chonderi, to Pegu, to Imahay in the kingdome of Siam, and back to Pegu, and from thence to Malacca, Zeilan, Cochin, and all the coast of the East India'. The reader is promised that 'the strange rites, maners, and customs of those people, and the exceeding rich trade and commodities of those countries are faithfully set downe and diligently described, by . . . M. Ralph Fitch'.

Unfortunately, the narrative itself is plain, with little colour and no emotion. Its sparseness is made even more irritating by the fact that so little is known of Fitch himself.

He was undoubtedly a merchant, but that is the only certain thing about him. There is no record of his birth, and the date of his death is open to question. From his few words emerges the picture of a sharp observer and a courageous man. But there are no really personal details. Fitch does not even explain how he managed—on what must have been a very small initial amount of money—to wander alone for four years across northern India, take ship to Burma and Malaya, and finally get back to England again.

This reticence may well have been an aspect of Fitch's own character. More probably, it was the editorial censorship of Richard Hakluyt, whose purpose in compiling his volumes was to give information, scientific, topographical and commercial, a purpose stuck to so ruthlessly that Fitch is not permitted to describe in any detail the architecture of the towns he passed through, or the faces of the great men he saw. It is unlikely that Fitch kept notes on his journeyings. Some of his information is openly taken from other travellers such as the Venetian, Cesar Federici, but most of the observations are obviously his own, and these, allowing for the inhibitions of an Englishman of his time—his conventional Christian view of the heathen, for example—are shrewd and sometimes witty appraisals of an exotic reality. No doubt Fitch enlarged upon them in conversations with the merchants who had sent him on his travels, and those anxious to know of the trade potential of India and beyond from a man with the same down-to-earth commercial standards as themselves. Certainly, what he had to say added yet another inducement for the merchants of London to extend their business to the East Indies, founding for their purpose a Company which after many vicissitudes became, as the East India Company, the ruler of India. Though Fitch has been claimed as a pioneer of Empire, it is well to keep in mind that neither he nor his sponsors had more in *their* minds than a purely commercial venture.

In telling the story of Fitch's travels there are considerable obstacles. Because of the absence of personal material, Fitch himself inevitably remains a shadowy figure. In that area his reticence is impenetrable. But on other levels it is not. The gaps in his narrative can be filled in from contemporary sources, both European and Asian. This is the method adopted here. Fitch's own words are used wherever possible. Their spelling has been modernised, but archaic forms have been retained so that at least some of the flavour of the original remains. The same applies to quotations originally written in or translated into Elizabethan or Jacobean English. A full list of these quotations and their sources is given at the end of the book.

Contents

	Preface	*page* 7
I	In search of spices	15
II	The road to Ormuz	21
III	Golden Goa	29
IV	Diamonds and idolaters	46
V	The court of the Great Mogul	62
VI	A rich and prosperous country	78
VII	Lord of the White Elephant	96
VIII	Gateway to Cathay	125
IX	The journey home	142
X	Charter for empire	156
	Appendix Ralph Fitch: his itinerary 1583/91	171
	Bibliography	173
	Notes on sources	175
	Index	181

Illustrations

PLATES

1. The trade of Syria in the sixteenth century. Loading up a camel caravan. *facing page* 48
2. General view of Goa. 48
3. The market place of Goa, slave auction in process 49
4. The Inquisition in Goa 49
5. The ramparts of Bijapur. Detail from a seventeenth-century painting showing Aurangzeb at the siege of Bijapur. 64
6. Woman worshipping an 'idol' (*lingam*) at a Shiva shrine. Painting, c. 1550, from Mandu. 64
7. European view of a suttee. 65
8. The queen of Golconda gathering diamonds, a fourteenth-century view. 65
9. Building the Red Fort, Agra. Mogul painting, c. 1600 112
10. Jesuits and Muslim theologians debating before the Emperor Akbar. 112
11. Malacca in the mid-sixteenth century. 113
12. Macao c. 1636. 113
13. Portuguese ship taking the first traders and missionaries to Japan. 128
14. Pepper harvest in Malabar, a late mediaeval view. 129
15. Beginning of the Charter of the first English East India Company. 129

ILLUSTRATIONS

Maps

Itinerary through Near East, 1583 and 1590/91 *page* 22
Itinerary in India and Further Asia, 1583/90 *pages* 54–55

I

In search of spices

In 1581, four merchants of the City of London—Sir Edward Osborne, Richard Staper, Thomas Smith and William Garret—received from Queen Elizabeth I letters patent under the title of 'The Company of Merchants of the Levant'.

'Her Majesty', read the Charter, 'grants unto those four merchants and to such other Englishmen, not exceeding twelve in number, as the said Sir E. Osborne and Staper shall appoint to join them and their factors, servants and deputies, for the space of seven years to trade with Turkey.' Both parties hoped for substantial returns, and not only in purely economic terms, for this was a period in which trade and diplomacy, commerce and politics, were inseparable. Indeed, written into the Queen's Charter was the proviso that the Company would hold the exclusive right to trade with Turkey only for as long as it did not 'appear to be unprofitable to the kingdom'.[1]

The alliance between Queen and merchant, the good of the state and the profits of trade, was underlined by the new company's first venture. Aboard the ship *Great Susan* when it left England in 1582 was William Harborne, plenipotentiary of the Queen and agent of the Levant Company. This dual role was not a new one for Harborne. In 1578 he had been sent to Constantinople by Osborne and Staper to obtain the right to trade in the Sultan's dominions. To escape the eyes of competitors, the Venetians who then had much of the Levant trade in their grasp and the French who already held privileges, Harborne had travelled overland through Poland and arrived in Constantinople, disguised in Turkish dress, in the train of a Turkish envoy returning home. While there, Harborne passed on letters from Elizabeth I to the Sultan and, in 1580, obtained the trade privileges Osborne and Staper had hoped for. Harborne's return to England had been immediately followed by the formation of the Company.

Harborne also brought back letters and information for the Queen. England was being threatened on every side by the power of Philip II of Spain. After Elizabeth's excommunication by the Pope in 1570, every Catholic conspiracy seemed to have Spain's hand behind it. Abroad, areas of profitable trade were cut off from the English. Their traditional markets in Europe were disturbed by the activities of the Spanish. The Americas were denied them. The sea route to the East Indies, so profitably discovered by the Portuguese, now after Philip's seizure of the throne of Portugal in 1580 fed the coffers of Spain. The Queen and her ministers were preoccupied with a search for allies among the enemies of Spain, the Dutch, the French, Don Antonio—the Portuguese claimant—and the Sultan of Turkey, still a formidable naval and military power. Elizabeth could do no more than encourage those merchants and adventurers who sought new ways of reaching Asia, that treasure mine where England's main export, woollen cloth, it was thought might be exchanged for all the luxuries of the East.

The English had learned a great deal about the potentialities of the East India trade. The Portuguese who had first made the long sea journey around Africa and across the Indian Ocean, while jealously guarding the secrets of that road and protecting it with their own forts and victualling stations along the way, had not concealed its riches. At the markets of Lisbon and later of the middlemen at Antwerp were displayed the gold, silver, pearls, dyes, fine cloths and, above all, the strong-flavoured aromatic spices that the palate of northern Europeans craved so much. This hunger for spices is, perhaps, a little difficult to understand in today's world in which everything is available at the supermarket in the High Street. But the wealthy of northern Europe four hundred years ago lived mainly on salt meat from autumn until spring. Even when fresh meat appeared once again in the summer it was poor in quality and lacking in flavour. Spices were more than a culinary delight, however. Because they were expensive, their use was an indication of affluence. The rich needed their pepper just because they *were* rich, and they were prepared to pay heavily for it.

English merchants had bought their stocks at Lisbon or Antwerp but, as with all merchants, were anxious to cut out the middlemen. For years Englishmen tried to penetrate the secrets of Portuguese navigation. Papers from captured Spanish and Portuguese ships were carefully collected. The secret agents of the court intercepted correspondence. But it took time to gather sufficient information to attempt the hazardous journey round Africa. In the meanwhile, other routes were explored. There was the north-east passage with Russia as the starting point—but the adventurers got no further. There was the north-west passage, but that too foundered on the Atlantic coast of Canada. Francis Drake, to prove that the calculated propaganda of the Spanish and Portuguese was a fiction, sailed through the straits of Magellan to circumnavigate the world. Others, putting more faith in the land route, braved the dangers of the Mediterranean infested with pirates to explore the way from the ports of the Levant to those of the Persian Gulf.

Among the pioneers were John Eldred, who made the difficult journey from Aleppo to Baghdad and lived in the latter city for two years, and John Newbery, who reached as far as the Portuguese trading station of Ormuz—the gateway to India—and spoke Arabic well. Only the next step, from Ormuz to India, remained.

It was Newbery's return to England in August 1582 which inspired Osborne and Staper to finance an attempt on that next step. Newbery had successfully concealed his identity from the Portuguese at Ormuz, and had come to the conclusion that an onward journey was possible. His knowledge of the routes to the Persian Gulf was unrivalled and he was the obvious choice to head the expedition. A number of merchants were chosen to take part. John Eldred (also for his experience of the terrain) and Ralph Fitch, who had no eastern experience but whose qualities were presumably well known to Osborne and Staper, were among them. Accompanying the party were two men, William Leedes, a jeweller, and James Story, a painter, chosen perhaps because it was known that eastern kings, and in particular the Mogul emperor, welcomed European craftsmen. It was at least one way of acquiring a friend at court. Of these five, four—except for some doubtful figures of the Middle Ages—were to be the first Englishmen to penetrate to the heart of India. One, Ralph Fitch, went deeper, journeying to the threshold of further Asia, to Burma and Malacca where no Englishman had ever been before.

The plans for the expedition were carefully thought out, and like all good plans were essentially simple. A ship would be fitted out and trade goods loaded. Two of the merchants were to remain at Baghdad with some of the stock and two more at Basra with more goods, while Newbery and Fitch would continue the journey to the Indies. To give them some diplomatic standing, Newbery was supplied with two letters from the Queen. One was addressed to the Mogul emperor, Akbar, called by the Elizabethans 'Zelabdim Echebar' (Jalaluddin Akbar), King of Cambaia (Cambay), and the other—just on the off-chance—to the emperor of China. In an age of discovery, it was worth preparing for eventualities. Elizabeth issued such letters sometimes without a superscription, for possible delivery to any important ruler her adventurers might happen to meet.

Under the circumstances, the sentiments expressed could be no more than vague; but there was no hesitation about asking for favours or giving promises of something in return:

> Elizabeth, by the grace of God . . . To the most invincible and most mighty Prince, Lord Zelabdim Echebar, King of Cambaia; Invincible Emperor . . . The great affection which our Subjects have to visit the most distant places of the world (not without good will and intention to introduce the trade of merchandise of all nations whatsoever they can; by which means the mutual and friendly traffic of merchandise on both sides may come), is the cause that the bearer of this letter, John Newbery, jointly with those that be in his company, with a courteous and honest boldness do repair to the borders and countries of your Empire. We doubt not but that your Imperial Majesty, through your royal grace, will favourably and friendly accept him. And that you would do it the rather for our sake, to make us greatly beholding to your Majesty, we should more earnestly and with more words require it if we did think it needful. But by the singular report that is of your Imperial Majesty's humanity in these uttermost parts of the world we are greatly eased of that burden, and therefore we use the fewer and less words. Only we

request that because they are our subjects they may be honestly entreated and received and that in respect of the hard journey which they have undertaken to places so far distant it would please your Majesty with some liberty and security of voyage to gratify it, with such privileges as to you shall seem good. Which courtesy if your Imperial Majesty shall to our subjects at our requests perform, We, according to our Royal Honour, will recompense the same with as many deserts as we can.

And herewith we bid your Imperial Majesty to fare well.[2]

How hard a journey it was to be for John Newbery, the Queen could not suspect, but of the four Englishmen who reached India, only Ralph Fitch was to return to England.

II

The road to Ormuz

The little group of merchants and the hopes of the Levant Company set sail in the ship *Tyger* from the Pool of London on 12 February 1583. Unfavourable winds kept the travellers off the coast of England until 11 March when, with the port of Falmouth disappearing over the horizon, they set sail for the Straits of Gibraltar and the dangers of the Mediterranean—that 'great sea of pirates'. But there were dangers even on the way, for on the thirteenth day out the winds changed once again, blowing up into a great storm which lasted for more than a week. 'In this great storm', wrote Newbery, 'we had some of our goods wet but God be thanked, no great hurt done.'[1] It was to be the worst part of the journey for, past the straits, the winds were fair and the pirates preoccupied elsewhere. The last day of April found the *Tyger* lying off the harbour of Tripoli in what is, today, the Lebanon.

Early next morning the party landed on St George's Island, 'a place where Christians dying aboard ships are wont to be buried',[2] and 'went a-maying'. Perhaps on this May Day, after a safe journey, the travellers felt that to indulge in the rural revels of home—on soil full, at least, of Christian bones—in the land of the pagan, was both a thanksgiving and a reassurance. Afterwards, they made their way to the *Fondeghi Ingles*, a large house 'builded of

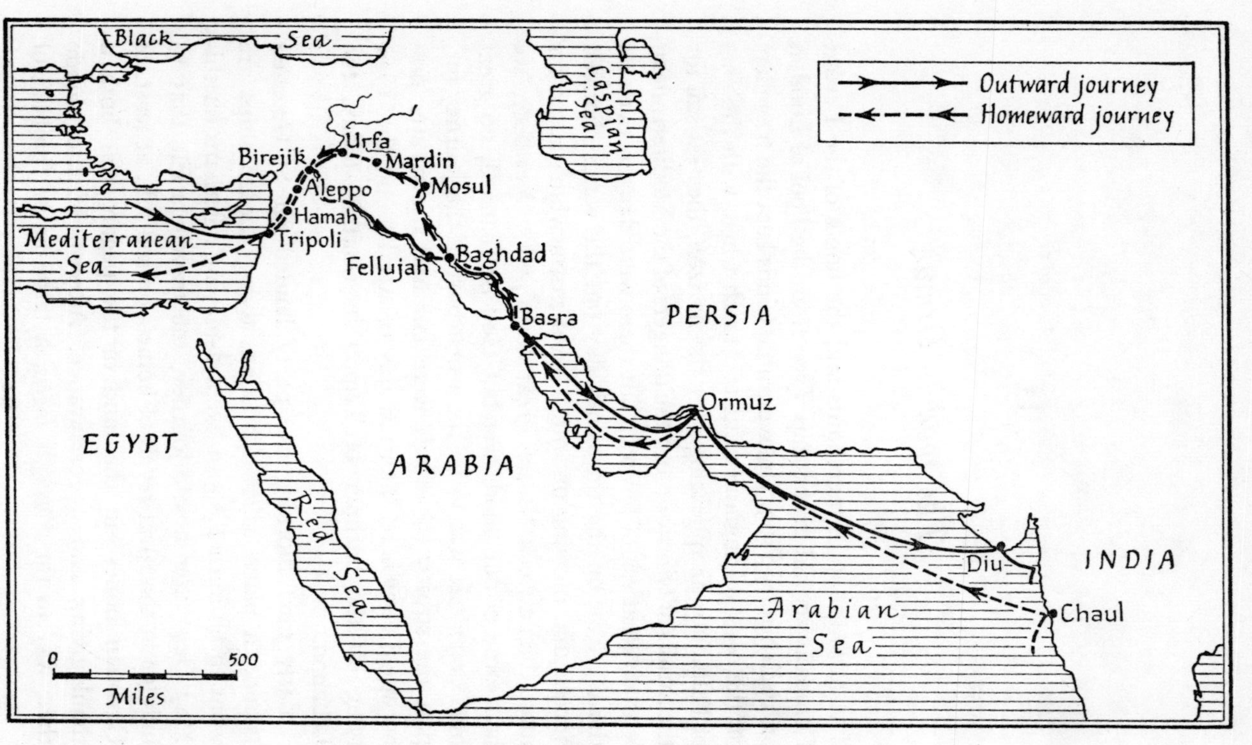

Itinerary through Near East, 1583 and 1590/91

stone like a Cloister',[3] where the English consul lived together with the English merchants of the town. All the foreign merchants lived in this way, in their own hostels, their flags flying on the roof, their goods displayed in the warehouse.

The hostels of the merchants were at the portside. The town of Tripoli lay some two miles away, surrounded by a wall and dominated by a strong fort. Through the town ran a river bounded by gardens of mulberry trees, 'on which there grow abundance of silkworms wherewith they make a great quantity of white silk, which is the chiefest natural commodity to be found in and about this place'.[4] But the new arrivals were not interested in doing business in Tripoli; the Company's agents were already well established there. The first important stopping place for Fitch and his companions on the journey to the Persian Gulf was the town of Aleppo.

This great international market was the centre for luxury goods, precious stones, diamonds and rubies, fine pearls and jade, costly perfumes and fragrant gums, musk and myrrh, all the spices of India and Arabia. 'Jews, Tartarians, Persians, Armenians, Egyptians, Indians and many sorts of Christians' traded there, as the local government allowed them to 'enjoy freedom of their consciences' and to 'bring thither many kinds of rich merchandises'.[5] The English had a consul there, and merchants in a fair way of business. It was Newbery's intention to sell some of the merchandise brought out on the *Tyger* and to buy goods 'to carry to Basra and the Indies'.[6]

The party stayed in Aleppo for ten days, Newbery reporting on the state of trade there and making recommendations to the Company in London. For the journey they purchased a quantity of coral and amber, and for small gifts to smooth the way, some soap and 'broken glass'[7] for beads and ornaments. On 31 May, dressed in Turkish clothing and riding upon camels, they set off for Birejik on the river Euphrates, from where they would sail down to Baghdad. Birejik was an important way-station on the trade route. Sixteen large ferryboats were permanently kept there and convoys of as many as five thousand camels were a commonplace. The party arranged for a small flat-bottomed boat to carry them and their goods down river to Fellujah. The boat had been bought, not hired. 'These boats be but for one voyage, for the stream doth run so fast downwards that they cannot return.'[8] On arrival at Fellujah they would have to sell the boat at a considerable loss, for, Fitch recorded, 'that which cost you fifty at Birejik you sell there for seven or eight'.[9]

The journey itself was risky. It was wise to stop at night but to stay on board and on guard, 'for the Arabians . . . will come swimming and steal your goods and flee away'.[10] Eldred, in fact, lost a casket, 'with things of good value in the same, from under my man's head as he was asleep'.[11] The thieves of the night were the food suppliers of the day, bringing butter and eggs, milk and lambs, in exchange for coral and amber and glass beads, 'for they care not for money'.[12] The men, with their light hair and skin, reminded the party of gipsies; so did the women, each with a nose ring of gold, silver or iron.

Except for the loss of Eldred's casket, the travellers found the journey uneventful, and they reached Fellujah on 28 June. A village of some hundred houses, Fellujah was merely a disembarkation point for those making their way to Baghdad, some fifty miles away on the bank of another river, the Tigris. It was the height of the hot season and the camel owners were unwilling to rent their beasts for the journey across the desert to Baghdad. But they were equally unwilling to lose profit, so a hundred asses were hired to carry the

English merchants and their goods. 'Travelling by night and part of the morning to avoid the great heat',[13] they arrived at Baghdad. Eldred knew the town well, so too did Newbery. But to Fitch everything was new. The bridge across the Tigris, 'made of boats and tied to a great chain of iron, which is made fast on either side of the river'. The rafts of air-filled goatskins covered with boards, floated down 'from Armenia', which after discharging their cargo were deflated and sent back by camel 'to serve another time'. There were less prosaic wonders, too. The 'Tower of Babel'—as it was thought to be—'which tower is ruinated on all sides and with the fall thereof hath made, as it were a mountain, so that it hath no shape at all'. Then, some two days' journey from Baghdad, there was a hole in the ground 'that doth continually throw forth against the air, boiling pitch'. It was known locally as the 'mouth of Hell'.[14]

Baghdad had its problems as well as its attractions. The party found difficulty in selling the goods they had brought with them—woollens, tin, and other things. A previous consignment from England, sent on from Aleppo, had saturated the market and there was no likelihood of selling the new stocks before winter. 'God send it to mend', wrote Eldred, 'or otherwise this Voyage of ours will make no profit.'[15] Leaving some of the stock at Baghdad, the party set out with the remainder for Basra.

Leaving Baghdad on 27 July, the party was barely half a day's journey down the river when the ship went aground. The river was low, and Newbery, fearing another catastrophe further down river, returned to Baghdad to hire a smaller vessel. The journey to Basra was completed without further incident ten days later.

Basra was a great centre of trade in spices and drugs which came mainly from India and farther east through the agency of the Portuguese at Ormuz. Surrounding the town were great fields of wheat and rice, and large orchards of date trees. Basra was not an altogether comfortable place for foreign traders. The local Turkish governor had a habit of fixing his own price for goods he wanted for himself, and it was not wise to reject his offer. Furthermore, if a foreigner was unfortunate enough to die in Basra, the governor would claim that the goods of the men who were with him were actually the property of the dead man and therefore subject to confiscation. Only a large bribe might convince him otherwise.

Eldred was to stay in Basra while Newbery, Fitch, Leedes and Story, with some of the stock, were to make for India. Newbery would have preferred to make the journey from Basra by sea to Bushire on the Persian Gulf, and then overland to India, but he lacked an interpreter and had to go to Ormuz. At Aleppo he had hired two men, one of whom spoke 'the Indian tongue and hath been twice there',[16] but they had turned out to be untrustworthy. 'My going to Ormuz', wrote Newbery to William Harborne in Constantinople, 'is more of necessity than for any goodwill I have to the place, for I want a man to go with me that hath the Indian tongue.'[17] The decision proved an unhappy one, for soon after their arrival he and his companions were arrested by the Portuguese and thrown into prison.

Ormuz was one of the most important of the trading stations set up by the Portuguese as part of their conquest of the Asian seas. From Ormuz at the mouth of the Persian Gulf, and from Diu and Goa on the west coast of India, the Portuguese dominated the trade of the Indian Ocean. Only one gap remained in the wall they had hoped to build in order to ensure that only through the doors they themselves controlled would the trade of the Indies penetrate to the Near East. In an attempt to seal off the Red Sea they had seized the island of Socotra, but this was too far away from the entrance. An attempt to take Aden failed. Nevertheless, at Ormuz they had acquired a growing concern, for it was already one of the richest entrepôts in the world when they took the island in 1515 and made its ruler their puppet.

Ormuz handled the spices of India and the Spice Islands of the Indonesian archipelago, fine silk from China, and sent back to India the pearls of the island of Bahrein, the rich carpets of Persia, and the Arab horses so much in demand for the armies of Indian princes. Naturally, its markets attracted to Ormuz merchants from all over the East. Of the Europeans, the most numerous were Venetians, and it was one of these, Michael Stropene—who had heard of the English from his brother in Aleppo—who denounced them to the Portuguese governor as spies.

No better way could have been found to destroy a potential competitor. The Venetians were aware of English intentions. Stropene had been suspicious of Newbery's earlier visit to Ormuz in 1581 and had enticed his Greek servant away in order, Newbery suspected, to pump him about his master's trade secrets.

The situation in Ormuz was ripe for accusations of espionage. Don Antonio, claimant to the throne of Portugal, had fled to England in 1581 after being defeated in battle by Philip of Spain. Orders had gone out to Goa to watch for signs of intrigues in the East on his behalf. When Stropene alleged that the Englishmen were spying for the pretender and had even brought with them a painter to draw plans of the fortifications of Ormuz, the governor—no doubt warned by the viceroy of Goa—was forced to listen. Stropene even reinforced his allegation by claiming that the English were heretics. In face of such a combination of charges, the governor could do nothing but take action, even though it appears that he was not unfriendly towards Newbery. He advised Newbery after his arrest to sell the goods he had brought with him and allowed him to leave prison in the morning to try to find buyers, provided he returned at night. This generosity did not prevent the governor from accepting 'a fountain of silver and gilt; six knives; six spoons and one fork trimmed with coral', five emeralds set in gold, and a number of yards of cloth, at less than half their value.[18]

This atmosphere of benevolence did not, however, help to relieve the Englishmen's minds about the future. Newbery was able to send out letters to Basra and Aleppo asking for help, but by the time it arrived they feared their throats might have been cut. Fitch was possibly unwell, for in a letter sent after their subsequent voyage to Goa he mentions that he had been 'sick of the flux', so sick that 'if we had stayed two days longer upon the water I think I had died'.[19] All Fitch records of the period in Ormuz is that he and his companions were in prison from 9 September until 11 October, and that they were then 'shipped for this city of Goa in the Captain's [i.e. the governor's] ship, with an hundred and fourteen horses and about two hundred men'.[20]

III

Golden Goa

The journey from Ormuz to Goa took twenty-four days. Travelling in the same vessel as the Englishmen was the former advocate-general of Ormuz, returning to Goa after his tour of duty. This important official called Newbery to his cabin and seems to have begun a preliminary interrogation. Newbery replied honestly to the questions and learned a little more about the reasons for his arrest. It was not, apparently, only a matter of Michael Stropene's denunciation. The visit of Francis Drake to the Spice Islands during his circumnavigation of the world some four years previously had upset the Portuguese. The advocate-general alleged that Drake, while in the Moluccas loading cloves, 'finding a galleon there of the King's of Portugal, he caused two pieces of his greatest ordnance to be shot at the same'. Newbery, 'perceiving that this did greatly grieve them . . . asked if they would be revenged of me for that which Master Drake had done. To which he answered, No; although his meaning was to the contrary.'[1]

The Englishmen had, in fact, a great deal to fear. The Drake affair obviously added an endorsement of guilt to the suggestion that they were spies. The Portuguese were particularly anxious for news of Don Antonio, the pretender, and of his intrigues with Elizabeth of England. Although Fitch and his companions knew nothing of this affair, it was quite possible that they might be tortured or even handed over as heretics to the Inquisition.

Whatever trepidation was in Fitch's mind, he did not forget the original purpose for which he had been sent on this journey. He noted that the trade in horses was so important to the Portuguese that, if a vessel carried both horses and goods, the latter entered without paying customs dues.

Fitch's first experience of India came at the Portuguese strongpoint of Diu, an island in the Gulf of Cambay which was used as an entrepôt for goods and as a base for Portuguese galleys controlling the access to the Persian Gulf. From Diu, the ship carrying the English travellers sailed to Daman, 'the second town of the Portugals in the country of Cambay',[2] where the trade was mainly in corn and rice.

Cambay was actually part of the formerly independent kingdom of Gujarat, whose ruler the Portuguese insisted on referring to as the 'King of Cambay' since the town was one of his chief residences. The Portuguese had been allowed to build a fort by the sultan Bahadur Shah in 1535 and had murdered him two years later by throwing him off one of their ships after he had been inveigled on board. Gujarat was now part of the empire of the Great Mogul, having been conquered in 1572 by Akbar, but the memory of at least one of the rulers was still green. This was Mahmud Begarha, who became a legend for his physical peculiarities. His beard reached his waist, and his alleged immunity to poison was to inspire the lines:

The Prince of Cambay's daily food
Is asp and basilisk and toad.
Which makes him have so strong a breath,
Each night he stinks a queen to death.[3]

After Daman, the next call was at Bassein, and then on to

Thana on the northern end of the island of Salsette. On 10 November they were at Chaul, a 'place of great traffic for all sorts of spices and drugs, silk and cloth of silk, sandals [sandalwood], elephants teeth [tusks], and much China work'. Here, too, perhaps, Fitch first learned of the virtues of the palm tree, 'the profitablest tree in the world. It doth always bear fruit, and doth yield wine, oil, sugar, vinegar, cord, coals; of the leaves are made thatch for the houses, sails for ships, mats to sit or lie on; of the branches they make their houses and brooms to sweep; of the tree, wood for ships'.[4]

Nine days later, on 29 November 1583, the Englishmen arrived at Goa, 'where for our better entertainment, we were presently put into a fair strong prison'.[5] Fitch does not say what the prison was like, nor even which one it was—Goa had several. It was obviously not the cells of that frightening institution, the Inquisition, for as yet there was no real suggestion that the Englishmen were heretics even though the suspicion must have been there in the minds of the Portuguese. Neither would it have been the personal prison of the Archbishop of the Indies, which was just as well, as it was a horrifying place in which the prisoners lay in their own dirt or, if they still had the strength, slept upright against a wall. It seems likely that Fitch and his companions were lodged in the main jail, the Sala das Bragas, next to the palace of the viceroy.

The Englishmen were first examined by a judicial officer who demanded their documents and alleged that they were spies for Don Antonio. This could not be proved. Possibly, in the hope of frightening them, the captives were afterwards interrogated about their religion—were they good Catholics or not? If not, it was probably implied, the doors of the Inquisition would close behind them.

Fitch and his companions, however, were not without

friends. Two in particular took an interest in their fate. Both were Jesuits. One was a Dutchman; the other, surprisingly enough, was English. Father Thomas Stevens had escaped from religious persecution in England to become a Jesuit in 1578. He was particularly attracted to the idea of saving the heathen in the Indies, and after persistently begging the general of his Order, was sent to Goa in the following year. By the time Fitch arrived, Stevens, known as Father Estavam, was recognised as a kind and generous man, a great preacher, and a scholar. In fact, he became one of the first Englishmen to study Indian languages, and certainly the first—and probably the last—to compose a great religious epic in one of them. His version of the Gospel story in Marathi, which he called the *Christian Purana*, is still popular reading today.

Not unnaturally, Father Stevens was concerned about the fate of his countrymen. With the help of the Dutch father and of Jan Linschoten, then a page in the service of the archbishop, he managed to persuade the viceroy to release the Englishmen, after finding 'sureties for us that we should not depart the country without the licence of the Viceroy'.[6]

While in prison, the four Englishmen had been under heavy pressure from the Jesuit fathers—with the exception apparently, of Stevens—to agree to join the Order in some lay capacity. Linschoten later alleged that the reason was that the Jesuits had learned that the Englishmen had a considerable sum of money with them as well as the trade goods they had been allowed to bring from Ormuz, and 'sought to get the same into their fingers; for that the first vow and promise they make at their entrance into their Order is to procure the welfare of the said Order, by what means soever it be'.[7] With Fitch, Newbery and Leedes the Jesuits failed, but the painter Story, 'partly for fear and partly for want of means to relieve himself, promised them to become a Jesuit'.[8] Though Story was not a merchant and had no claim on either the money or the goods, the Jesuits welcomed him because of his craft. There were very few European painters in India and the Jesuits saw the opportunity to have frescoes for their church painted on the cheap.

Story was released ten days before the others. Newbery was freed on 21 December, and Fitch and Leedes the following day. On the whole they had been lucky. Their stay in jail, though a frightening experience, had not been long. 'It doth spite the Italians to see us abroad', wrote Fitch in a letter of 24 January 1584, 'and many marvel at our delivery.'[9] But they still had to be careful.

Stevens had found them a citizen of Goa to stand as surety, and they had handed over in cash before their release half the surety of two thousand ducats, with a promise to pay the rest from the sale of their goods. In order to do this, with the help of friends they hired a house and shop in the principal street of the town and soon acquired a reputation for courtesy and honesty. They 'behaved themselves so discreetly that no man carried an evil eye—no, nor an evil thought—towards them. Which liked not the Jesuits', added Linschoten, 'because it hindered them from what they hoped for.'[10]

The house and shop stood on the Rua Direita, which ran from the palace of the viceroys to the church of the Misericordia. Neither Newbery nor Fitch bothered to describe the beautiful city they now found themselves free in. *Goa Dourada*, Golden Goa, was a cosmopolitan city on an island, the greatest European settlement in the East at that time, so rich and elegant with fine palaces and churches that there was even a proverb about it: *Quem vio Goa excusa de vēr Lisboa* ('whoever has seen Goa need not see Lisbon'). The

Rua Direita was lined on both sides with stately buildings where bankers, jewellers and many other traders carried on their business. The street was always crowded, especially during the mornings when auction sales were held. Linschoten describes the people of all creeds and races, with large umbrellas held over their heads to protect them from the strong sun or the monsoon rains. There, too, sales of the property of men condemned to death were held, and tax collectors had their counting houses. At one point there was a horse market, at another, slaves of both sexes were exhibited for sale. Many of these slaves, Linschoten noted, were skilled 'in music and embroidery and several other useful arts, and fetch a price proportionate to their accomplishments, no less than to their personal charms'.[11]

In fact, slaves played a very important role in the lives of the Portuguese in Goa. They did all the work in the house and were even trained to trade. The produce of the garden—worked by slaves—would be sold by slaves in the bazaar. Slaves would weave and dye cloth, also for sale. The prettier of the female slaves would become concubines. According to an observant Frenchman, the most favoured were negresses imported from Africa, 'wondrously black with curly hair'.[12] Even the great ladies were not above hiring out their female slaves as prostitutes. The market was constantly supplied not only with the more exotic specimens from abroad, but a very large business was done in kidnapping young boys and girls from the territories of Indian states. For the Portuguese, it was indeed Golden Goa, and even the common soldier had his slave.

The image of luxury, the Portuguese authorities believed, was an important factor in their rule. It was necessary for the Indians to believe that all Portuguese were superior. The soldiers might be ex-convicts—all were certainly from the lower classes—but as soon as they landed in India they became gentlemen. The soldiers aped their betters, even changing their names for more aristocratic ones. As there were no barracks, a dozen or so soldiers would rent a house, buy three or four elegant suits, and hire slaves to cook for and comfort them. The suits were worn in turn, the wearers of the day strutting out as if 'they were lords . . . such is their bravery, with their slaves behind them and a man carrying over them a big parasol'. When they met another of their kind, similarly bedecked and supported by retainers, they would indulge in a vast display of what they believed to be the manners of the nobility. While still some distance apart, Linschoten recorded, they began to 'stoop with their bodies, and to thrust forth their foot to salute each other, with their Hats in their hands, almost touching the ground'.[13] Each was ready to see a real or imagined insult—too few bows, or a compliment not quite extravagant enough. Such insults were rarely settled by duels between the two men. An ambush would be arranged and the offender beaten up. For a particularly vile insult, a slave might be ordered to deliver a stab in the back.

If a soldier was reasonably presentable, he could give up the shared life and clothes of a communal establishment for a more luxurious but uncertain one with a Eurasian mistress. Because Portugal was such a small country, there was a great shortage of manpower with which to run the empire. From the beginning, mixed marriages as well as less formal relationships were encouraged. By the end of the sixteenth century, Goa was full of half-caste women, all—it would seem—with a desire for a man of unmixed European blood. To get one, a woman would be prepared to support him, buy his clothes and give him pocket money. The uncertainty came if the man wanted to end the connection or was discovered to be unfaithful. If he was not very careful, he would be poisoned. What was the poison most used is not known, but at least two reliable witnesses, including Linschoten, testify that it might take as much as six months to act. The victim would seem in perfect health throughout that time but would then, without warning, drop down dead.

It would have been unlikely for Fitch, as a foreigner—and one out on bail, as well—to be invited into the houses of the upper classes, but he must have seen them in the streets, perhaps even the cavalcade of that great nobleman, the viceroy of the Indies, on one of his rare excursions outside his palace. The viceregal palace overlooked the river and was fronted by a square of elegant houses. From the square, a large stone staircase led up to the entrance hall. The hall was hung with pictures of all the ships which had come out to India since the time of the great navigator, Vasco da Gama, in 1498. From here the way led into another hall hung this time with life-size portraits of all the viceroys, with plaques retailing their dates, achievements, and exploits while in office. In this hall the viceroy received the ambassadors of the Indian rulers and other distinguished visitors.

The private apartments were decorated with equal luxury, the palace had its own private water reservoir, its own private chapels. The viceroy was paid a substantial salary, but his main purpose was to make a fortune during his usually short term of office. There were many ways in which he could do so. The ambassadors of Indian princes never came empty-handed. All the profitable offices of state were in the viceroy's gift and were never given away for nothing. No viceroy had been known to go home without, at least, a fortune equivalent to what today would be a million pounds sterling, and many left with more. Naturally, when such a resplendent personage left his palace, he went surrounded by the pomp and splendour suited to his office—and his expectations.

Early in the morning, the English merchants might have seen a gathering of gentlemen four hundred strong, mounted on fine Arabian stallions and each attended by a Muslim groom carrying a horse-tail whisk to ward off the flies. Ranged on the steps would be the viceregal guard, a hundred men in blue uniforms and gold lace, each carrying a bright steel halberd. Presently the viceroy, richly dressed, would emerge and mount his horse. As the cavalcade moved off, the bright sun would glisten on the gold and silver trappings, the pearls and precious stones. Over each horseman a footman in livery held a great parasol. But these were by no means all the attendants thought necessary to accompany the viceroy. Each horseman had his personal bodyguard of six very tall negroes carrying scimitars and wearing padded jackets which made them look enormous, as well as twelve pages dressed in silk. Behind the column came the palanquins, empty, available in case their owners should tire of riding.

The viceroy might be on his way to attend a festival at one of the religious houses, of which Goa boasted more than fifty. Perhaps the most important of the celebrations was that of the saint's day of Francis Xavier, Apostle of the Indies, whose mummified body then lay in the church of St Paul. As well as the church there was a college which had been established in 1542 for the purpose of teaching new Asian converts to Christianity not only the art of preaching the gospel but some knowledge of the arts and science.

Francis Xavier had arrived in Goa in the year in which the college was founded and had taken up residence there two years later. His appearance had both shocked and excited the Portuguese. Unlike other great churchmen—and Xavier was both representative of the King of Portugal, and papal nuncio—he stepped ashore amid the great throng of richly dressed nobles and priests wearing a coarse woollen habit ragged at the edges. His feet were bare, but he refused to be carried in a palanquin and walked to the archbishop's palace. On his arrival there he asked for the hospital and, when he reached it, began to wash the sores of the lepers.

Some Portuguese approved—and maintained that they had seen a halo around Xavier's head. Others complained that he was letting down the image of Portuguese superiority. But Xavier continued his mission in the way he had always intended. Barefoot and in rags, he tended the sick, prayed with prisoners in their dungeons. The Portuguese in Goa, shamed by Xavier's saintly ways, began to give up their violent, luxurious life and to worry instead about the state of their souls. A more permanent result, however, was a wave of church building which was to give Goa much of its air of luxury.

Satisfied, it seems, by the reformation of the Portuguese in Goa, Xavier left to embark on the main object of his mission—the conversion of the heathen. He concentrated upon ordinary people, identifying their sufferings with their separation from the love of the true God. Black of beard and eye, his feet bare and his robe tattered, his personality radiating a convincing passion, he could not have chosen a more Asian way of reaching the hearts of those he wished to save, for they were the hallmark of the holy man throughout the East. Xavier's mission took him as far as Japan, but he never reached China, dying in 1552 on an island in the estuary of the Canton river.

Xavier died alone except for one follower, a Chinese Christian who had taken the name of Antonio de Santa Fe. Antonio buried his master in a shallow grave, and to save it from the jackals covered the body with lime to destroy it. When the news reached the Portuguese settlement of Malacca, it was decided to send an expedition to exhume the body. The party arrived three months after Xavier's death—and found the corpse in an almost perfect state of preservation. This was taken as a miracle, well in keeping with Xavier's saintly reputation. The body was still fresh, the cheeks still pink, when the coffin was opened on its arrival at Goa to be deposited in the Jesuit college of St Paul. Once a year thereafter the body was exposed, a large number of people being allowed to approach and kiss the feet. On the first occasion one pilgrim, Isabel de Carom, bit off a toe and carried it away in her mouth.

Ralph Fitch would certainly have seen the great ladies of Goa at church, but nowhere else, for the Portuguese kept their women in almost oriental seclusion. Yet they managed to deceive their husbands just the same. Their allies were their servants and the drug datura, a narcotic of the nightshade variety which, though a deadly poison in quantity, could be used in small doses to dull a man's mind so that he was not aware of what was going on under his eyes. The datura would be put into a drink or a bowl of soup, and an hour afterwards the husband became 'giddy and insensible, singing, laughing and performing a thousand antics'. Under the influence of the drug, men 'lost all consciousness and judgement. Then do the wives make use of their time, admitting whom they will, and taking their pleasure in the presence of their husbands who are aware of nothing.'[14] When the effects of the drug had worn off the husbands had no recollection of what had happened, and did not even know that they had been drugged.

When a great lady went to church she was, of course, on her best behaviour and as remote as possible. Dressed in gold and silver brocade, adorned with pearls and precious stones, bristling with jewellery, her head covered by a veil of fine crêpe which reached to her feet, she would arrive in her palanquin with a score of maidservants. Sometimes the palanquin would be carried right into the church. One of the servants bore a rich carpet, another costly cushions, a third 'a China gilt chair, a fourth a velvet case containing a book, a handkerchief and other necessary things, a fifth a very thin beautiful mattress to be spread over the carpet and a sixth a fan'.[15] When she walked, a Portuguese lady had to be assisted, for it was fashionable to wear *chopines*, shoes with a sole six inches thick. Leaning on the arms of two footmen, her progress was slow and dignified. It took perhaps as much as fifteen minutes to cover twenty yards. Once in her place with her maids around her, her eyes—in a highly painted face—meekly downcast, the lady would tell her beads in the soft undersea light which came through the windows. In Goa glass was not used. The window frames were filled with mother-of-pearl.

The English found much to see in Goa but they were still under restraint and the threat of further action against them. The Jesuits were still trying to persuade Newbery, Fitch and Leedes to join Story and 'yield themselves Jesuits into their cloister'. In return they were promised protection. The priests told them that they would have been sent to Lisbon, if only there had been a ship to take them. An approach to the viceroy for release from their sureties brought a threatening reply—if they were not careful, they would find themselves subjected to the *strappado*. This torture consisted of tying the victim's hands behind his back and hoisting him up by a rope fastened to them; the rope was then released and jerked taut again when the victim had begun to fall, the terrible wrench almost pulling his arms from the socket.

The Englishmen were now faced with an open threat of torture, the *strappado* in Goa, or worse perhaps in Lisbon. They had so far escaped the attentions of the Inquisition in Goa, but they might not be so fortunate in the capital of Portugal. There is little doubt that Fitch and his companions knew what they might expect if they fell into the hands of the Inquisitors. The Jesuits would not fail to enlarge on the terrors which waited behind the black stone façade of the Palace of the Inquisition, such a short distance away from the Englishmen's shop in the Rua Direita. In its great hall, a huge crucifix stood against the wall. The people of Goa believed that anyone charged with witchcraft or any other offence against the Catholic faith would, if brought before this giant cross, tremble violently and then faint, unable to keep his eyes on the figure of Christ.

The Inquisition was greatly feared in Goa, as elsewhere, because a charge of heresy could rarely be disproved. The Inquisition was mainly concerned with the converted, particularly with Jews who, in order to be able to trade in Goa, had declared themselves Christians. If they were poor, they were usually left alone; as all the goods of a suspect were immediately confiscated, it was obviously more profitable to arrest the rich. But anyone, high or low, Portuguese or foreigner, might find his shoulder tapped one day by a Familiar who informed him that he was arrested on a charge of heresy. Then, unless a man had powerful friends who were prepared to take the risk of interceding for him, he could find himself facing a case concocted after his arrest. 'Nothing in the world is more cruel and pitiless than the procedure,' wrote a Frenchman at the beginning of the seventeenth century. 'The least suspicion, the slightest word, whether of a child or of a slave who wishes to do his master a bad turn, is enough . . . they give credence to a child however young, so only he can speak.' Naturally, when a man was arrested, 'there is no friend will dare say a word for him'.[16]

Once a man was inside a cell, the Inquisitor's aim was to break his spirit. Often, he was not informed of the precise nature of the charges against him or of who had denounced him. The techniques were not very different from those familiar to us today in the psychological methods of the secret police in many countries, and were remarkably effective. The sentence, when it finally came, might be death by burning at the stake, or condemnation to the galleys in Portugal for a period of years. Expiation of one kind or other came at a ceremony known as an *auto-da-fé*, an 'act of faith' which took place usually every two years at Advent. This was made as terrifying for the condemned as it possibly could be.

Very early in the morning the prisoners would be awakened in the prison of the Inquisition and assembled to put on special clothes. All wore a black-and-white striped robe down to the ankles. Those condemned for offences against the Catholic faith had over this a short, sleeveless smock known as a *sanbenito*, made of yellow cloth with a St Andrew's cross on it in red. Those condemned to death wore a grey *sanbenito* painted with devils, flames, and burning firebrands surrounding a portrait of themselves. On their head was placed a cone of paper like a dunce's cap, also with devils and flames painted on it. After hours of waiting the prisoners would march in procession behind the standard of the Inquisition, an embroidered representation of the founder, St Dominic, holding a sword in one hand and, in the other, an olive branch, with the inscription 'Justicia et Misericordia'.

The service that followed at the church of St Francis of Assisi was attended by the viceroy and other dignitaries.

Each prisoner had with him a sponsor known as his Father in God. This was a citizen of Goa who walked with the prisoner to the church, sat with him during the service, and presented him at the end. To be Father in God to a penitent was considered an honour by all classes in Goa. At the end of the service, and after an improving sermon, the judgements were read out. All included excommunication from the Church, but those not sentenced to death were absolved by the touching of their breasts with a wand. Those condemned to execution were handed over to the civil authority with a request for mercy or, if that were not possible, death without the shedding of blood. There was no appeal against the sentence of the Inquisition, and the civil authority would not have dared to show mercy. In fact, all had been arranged beforehand and the viceroy and his staff made their way to a selected spot on the bank of the river that divided the city of Goa from the mainland and settled down to watch the burning.

The Englishmen may have missed this edifying spectacle during their stay in Goa, but they must have been fully aware of the danger in which they stood from both the civil and the religious authorities. The viceroy might pack them off to Lisbon on a charge of spying for Don Antonio; an enemy among the traders of Goa might denounce them to the Inquisition. Their surety, one Andreas Taborer, was demanding more money.

Under the circumstances, it seemed wiser to break their parole, even at the cost of losing money and goods. The decision made, they began to convert such money as they had managed to save or keep into precious stones. When the time was right, Fitch, Newbery and Leedes, taking with them food and drink, went to a spot some three miles from Goa ostensibly on a shooting expedition. Behind them in the

Rua Direita they left the house and shop with its unsold goods in the care of a Dutch boy who had been found for them by Jan Linschoten.

No one seems to have guessed the Englishmen's intentions. They told no one, not even men like Father Stevens and Linschoten who had befriended them. Linschoten says they hired as a guide an Indian courier who 'in the Winter times' carried 'letters from one place to another',[17] but Fitch in his narrative claims they had no guide, 'for we durst trust none'.[18] This, under the circumstances, seems more likely. After two days' walking they began to feel safer, for by then they had reached the dominions of the sultan of Bijapur.*

When the departure of the English became known, there was a 'great stir and murmuring among the people'[19] and it was suggested that Linschoten had been responsible for advising them to leave. Shortly afterwards, Andreas Taborer seized the goods they had left behind and handed money gained from their sale to the viceroy. 'The flight of the Englishmen', wrote Linschoten, 'grieved the Jesuits most, because they lost their prey.'[20] They even lost James Story, although he had been left behind. Story, claiming he had made no binding promise to stay with the Jesuits and had no desire to do so, hired a house and opened a shop where he did good business with his paintings. Within a short time he married a Eurasian. Nothing further is known about him, but it is possible that he was drowned at sea.

News of the English captives had reached King Philip of

*There is some uncertainty about the date of departure from Goa of Fitch and his two companions. Fitch gives 5 April 1585, which would mean that the party stayed sixteen months in the city, but Linschoten throws doubt on this by mentioning, by implication, a period of only five months. At least one historian thinks that Fitch made a slip and really meant 1584, but there is no contributory evidence for this. The slip could as easily have been five months for fifteen. In this book I have preferred Fitch's own dates.

Spain some time in 1584. In February 1585 he wrote to the viceroy at Goa to say that if they were found guilty they must be punished, and to advise him to keep a sharp eye open for any other Englishmen who might try to enter Goa. When he heard from the viceroy that the Englishmen had escaped from the city, the king wrote, in 1587 and again in 1589, urging the authorities to do everything they could to recapture them and to punish anybody who had helped them escape. Two years later, he ordered that Story should be sent to Lisbon. There is no surviving record to confirm whether or not this was done, but if it was, the painter probably perished in one of the two ships which disappeared on their way to Portugal in 1592.

IV

Diamonds and idolaters

The three Englishmen must have moved away as fast as possible from the vicinity of Goa, for the Portuguese might well have pursued them into the dominions of the sultan of Bijapur. Fitch does not mention it, but they would undoubtedly have adopted Indian dress to make themselves less conspicuous; the state of Bijapur was not particularly friendly toward the Portuguese, and it would have been difficult to explain to someone who had never heard of England that there was a difference between men from England and men from Portugal. The Englishmen could pass themselves off as merchants—from Persia, perhaps, which would account for their light complexions and the colour of their eyes. Newbery, we know, already spoke Arabic; Fitch could hardly have travelled as he did if he had not acquired some Indian tongue.

The party arrived first at the town of Belgaum, where there was 'a great market kept, of Diamonds, Rubies, Sapphires'[1] and other precious stones. Though it is possible the Englishmen did some business there—perhaps purchasing precious stones with such money as they had not already been able to convert into gems during their stay in Goa—Belgaum was too near Portuguese territory for comfort. Fitch, Newbery and Leedes seem to have reached the city of Bijapur, from which the state took its name, before the end of April 1585. They were now really in India. Not the India of the Portuguese, but the India of the Indians. How much the party knew of political conditions is not clear. They had left England with all the information that was available there—which was not very much—and they must have taken the opportunity of learning what they could during their stay in Goa.

They can hardly have been unaware that the Great Mogul, Akbar—to whom their queen's letter was addressed—did not rule the whole of India. Across the waist of the sub-continent lay a number of states ruled by Muslim sultans, descendants of earlier Muslim invaders than the Moguls, who had arrived in India only with Akbar's grandfather, Babur, in 1525. Much of the sultans' time was taken up with fighting amongst themselves, although twenty years before Fitch's arrival they had come together to attack the last remaining Hindu empire, that of Vijayanagar, which dominated the southern tip of India. When they were not fighting, the sultans spent their resources on building palaces and magnificent tombs. Their courts were brilliant with poets and artists.

Bijapur was no exception, though Fitch would not see much, if anything, of the life of the court. The city itself he described as 'a very great town',[2] and left it at that. Considering the commercial purpose of the English venture, he might reasonably have been expected to discuss the markets at least, which appear to have been famous. According to another contemporary source, there was near the king's palace—a superb collection of 'lofty buildings, houses and porticoes'—a bazaar of considerable size, thirty yards wide and about three miles long. 'Before each shop was a beautiful green tree and the whole bazaar was extremely clean and pure. It was filled with rare goods, such as are not seen or heard of in any other town.'

Of these rare goods, brought by caravan from all parts of Asia, those in the jewellers' shops were naturally the most luxurious. There were 'jewels of all sorts, wrought into a variety of articles, such as daggers, knives, mirrors, necklaces, and also into the form of birds, parrots, doves and peacocks . . . all studded with valuable jewels, and arranged upon shelves, rising one above the other'. The tradesmen went in for attractive displays designed to catch the customer's eye. The jeweller obviously had a built-in advantage, but the baker and the cloth-seller did what they could with lesser materials. The vendor of spirits and perfumes arranged on his shelves 'various sorts of china vessels, valuable crystal bottles and costly cups, filled with choice and rare essences . . . while in the front of the shop were jars of double-distilled spirit'. The fruiterer's shop sold not only the musk melons and the pomegranates, the luscious mangoes, dates and figs and all the other fruits of the season, but also 'sweetmeats such as pistachio nuts, and sugar candy, and almonds'.

Jewellery, foods and cloths were not the only commodities available in the market. Appropriately, next to the wine merchant's shop there was an 'establishment of singers and dancers, beautiful women adorned with various kinds of jewel' and attended by musicians, 'all ready to perform whatever may be desired of them'. The streets of this paradisial market were filled with people, drinking in the wine shops, frequenting the houses of the courtesans, pricing a jewel, or a fine sword at the armourer's—all, according to this observer, happy, gay, and above all friendly, for 'none quarrelled or disputed with another, and this state of things was perpetual. Perhaps no place in the wide world could present a more wonderful spectacle to the eye of the traveller.'[3]

1. The trade of Syria in the sixteenth century. Loading up a camel caravan. From André Thevet *La Cosmographie Universelle* (Paris 1575). *By courtesy of the Trustees of the British Museum*, London.

2. General view of Goa. From C. Dellon *Nouvelle Relation d'un Voyage fait aux Indes Orientales* (Amsterdam 1699).

3. The market place of Goa, slave auction in process. From Jan Huygen van Linschoten *Histoire de la Navigation* (Amsterdam 1638).

4. The Inquisition in Goa. From C. Dellon *Relation de l'Inquisition de Goa* (Paris 1688).

Though he does not seem to have thought the bazaars of Bijapur worth mentioning, Fitch did note that there were many Hindus at the sultan's court. In fact, most of the population consisted of Hindus, 'great idolaters'.[4] The woods surrounding the city were full of 'idols which they call Pagodes'.[5] Obviously these 'Pagodes'—a word used indiscriminately by Fitch to describe both the temples and the images inside them—were of great interest to him. In his remarks on the religious practices of the lands he passed through, Fitch displayed the current piety of his countrymen and their general belief in the unfortunate attitudes of the heathen. Of the images he saw through the gates of the temples, some were 'like a cow, some like a monkey, some like buffaloes, some like peacocks and some like the devil'.[6] His comments were not always quite so harsh. In Chaul on his journey to Goa, he had seen people who worshipped the cow and had merely found this 'strange'.[7] He also noticed a sect—in fact, that of the Jains—who would kill no living thing 'nor have anything killed. In the town they have hospitals to keep lame dogs and cats, and for birds.'[8] He did not say whether or not he approved of them.

From Bijapur, Fitch and his companions marched north-east and into another of the sultanates, that of Golconda. Now they were moving through a land of fable well known to Europeans from the time of the Middle Ages and even before. Golconda was a synonym for diamonds, for which the area was famous. Again, Fitch, the down-to-earth merchant, mentions only that the stones were of the finest water. It was not for him to retell the old stories, or even to prove them wrong. Marco Polo in the thirteenth century had described the mountains of diamonds, from which the rain washed stones into the valleys where serpents of immense size prevented them from being collected. 'But I will tell you what men do. They take many lumps of flesh imbrued in blood and fling them down into the depths of the valley. And the lumps thus flung down pick up great numbers of diamonds, which become embedded in the flesh. Now it so happens that these mountains are inhabited by a great many white eagles . . . When these eagles spy the flesh lying at the bottom of the valley, down they swoop and seize the lumps and carry them off.'[9] The men, watching carefully, would then rush forward shouting to scare the eagles into dropping the diamond-studded meat before they could swallow it.

Many people in Europe still believed such inventive tales. Fitch presumably saw how the diamonds were collected and considered the method too prosaic to record. In fact, it was fairly simple. Of the two diamond fields in the Deccan, one had sandy soil. As the stones were near the surface, all that was necessary was to search and sift. At the other field, the diamonds were to be found in soil with a large proportion of clay which had to be washed away before sifting could take place. A merchant would mark out a plot of about half an acre and employ a large number of labourers to dig out the soil. Women and children would then carry the soil to a walled enclosure where it was covered with water brought in earthen pots. The mixture of water and clay was then allowed to run out through holes in the wall, leaving behind the sand which, when dry, was shaken in the baskets used to winnow grain at harvest time. The diamonds, usually embedded in larger pieces of sand and clay, remained behind and were picked over by hand. A later traveller recorded, perhaps with some little exaggeration, that as many as sixty thousand labourers were employed in the diamond fields.

The ruler of Golconda was Muhammad Kuli Kutb Shah, the last two words of his name being a title borne by all the rulers of the state and meaning 'pole star of the kingdom'. In Fitch's strange transliteration they take on the sound of some mediaeval French knight and emerge as 'Cutup de Lashash'. The city of Golconda, Fitch described with his characteristic understatement as 'pleasant, with fair houses of brick and timber; it aboundeth with great store of fruits and fresh water'.[10] As a later English traveller put it, Golconda was a 'city that for sweetness of air, conveniency of water, and fertility of soil' was 'accounted the best situated in India'.[11] The palace of the ruler, 'which for bigness and sumptuousness, in the judgement of such as have travelled India, exceedeth all belonging to the Mogul or any other Prince',[12] was built of stone embellished with marble and gilding.

Fitch makes no mention of the market of Golconda, nor, apart from the trade in diamonds, of its commerce. But he observes the people, and remarks that 'here the men and women do go with a cloth bound about their middles without any more apparel'.[13] This was probably true of the poor in most of India, even in the cold of the northern winter. Even the rich, if they were Hindus, often wore no more than a lower garment. But the women of the upper classes would wear a small tight bodice which left their stomachs bare, and Muslim officials were inevitably seen in the traditional long coat of fine muslin or other material. Hindus, at court, would wear the same.

Most of the early travellers, like Fitch, emphasised the nakedness of the Indians and paid little attention to the garments that were actually worn. In fact, foreigners would be unlikely to see how the women of the upper classes, Muslim or Hindu, were dressed, for these women were kept in some seclusion and travelled protected by the screens of their palanquins. One class of woman could, however, be observed at will. Some twenty years after Fitch, another English traveller in Golconda was to describe the 'Boga Waro . . . in English the Whores Tribe',[14] which specialised in producing girls for the profession of temple prostitute, 'from whence there never wants a sinful succession of impudent harlots, whom the laws of the country do both allow and protect'.[15] Once a year these women paid homage to the ruler at Golconda. Many of them were rich, dressed in fine cottons and silks 'so bound about them as that one part being made fast about the waist covereth downwards, another part comes over the head covering all that way'.[16] Underneath, the women wore 'a thin waistcoat that covereth their breasts and arms unto the elbow'.[17] In fact, this is a description of the choli and sari of today.

The chief port of Golconda 'which standeth eight day's journey hence toward the gulf of Bengala'[18] was Masulipatam, on the east coast of India. Fitch does not actually say whether he or any of the party visited the port, but he does record that many ships came there, not only from other parts of India but from Burma and Sumatra, 'very richly laden with pepper, spices and other commodities'.[19] There was also a substantial export trade to Mocha on the Red Sea, and to Ceylon. To Mocha, the ruler of Golconda sent a gift of rice for the pilgrims to the holy cities of Islam, Mecca and Medina, and there was trade in cloth, iron, indigo, and 'benjamin', a kind of incense made from benzoin which the Arabs called 'Java frankincense'—with some accuracy, for it came from Indonesia. It was brought from there to India, with the finest camphor, spices and other commodities, in ships returning after delivering cargoes of iron and steel, calicoes both plain and printed, and diamonds. The ships also brought for the luxury market fine porcelain from China, as well as silks, lacquer ware, and aromatic woods.

From Pegu in Burma came rubies and sapphires, gold, tin, and quicksilver, in return for cotton yarn and dyed cloth.

There was also a large coastal trade. With the Hindu kingdom of Vijayanagar there was brisk business in slaves—particularly in children. In fact, Masulipatam was an extremely important entrepôt for both the Indian and East Indian trade. Though Fitch did not stress its importance in his narrative, he must certainly have communicated his findings verbally to his employers when he returned home. When, some years later, the English first ventured into the India trade, Masulipatam was one of the first places they made for. A trading agency was established there in 1611, and twenty-three years later they received from the ruler of Golconda the famous 'golden firman' granting them certain privileges. The firman was so called because the sultan's seal was impressed upon a leaf of gold.

But in 1585 the little party of Englishmen, the first to appear in Golconda, were anxious not to waste time. Their aim was to reach Agra and the court of the Great Mogul. It was desirable to observe the possibilities of trade with lesser kings, but the main object of their journey lay many miles to the north.

From Golconda they made their way to a town Fitch calls Servidore. This was probably Shehrbidar, 'Bidar town', the capital of the sultanate of Bidar, whose king 'is called the King of Bread'.[20] What Fitch's readers must have made of this strange potentate is hard to guess. It is, once again, an example of the bizarre rendering of Indian names characteristic of travellers in exotic lands. The 'King of Bread' was the ruler of Bidar, Mirza Ali, who was one of the *Barid* Shahi dynasty. Bidar, too, was 'a fine country', but Fitch did not think very much of the people. Neither the Muslims nor the

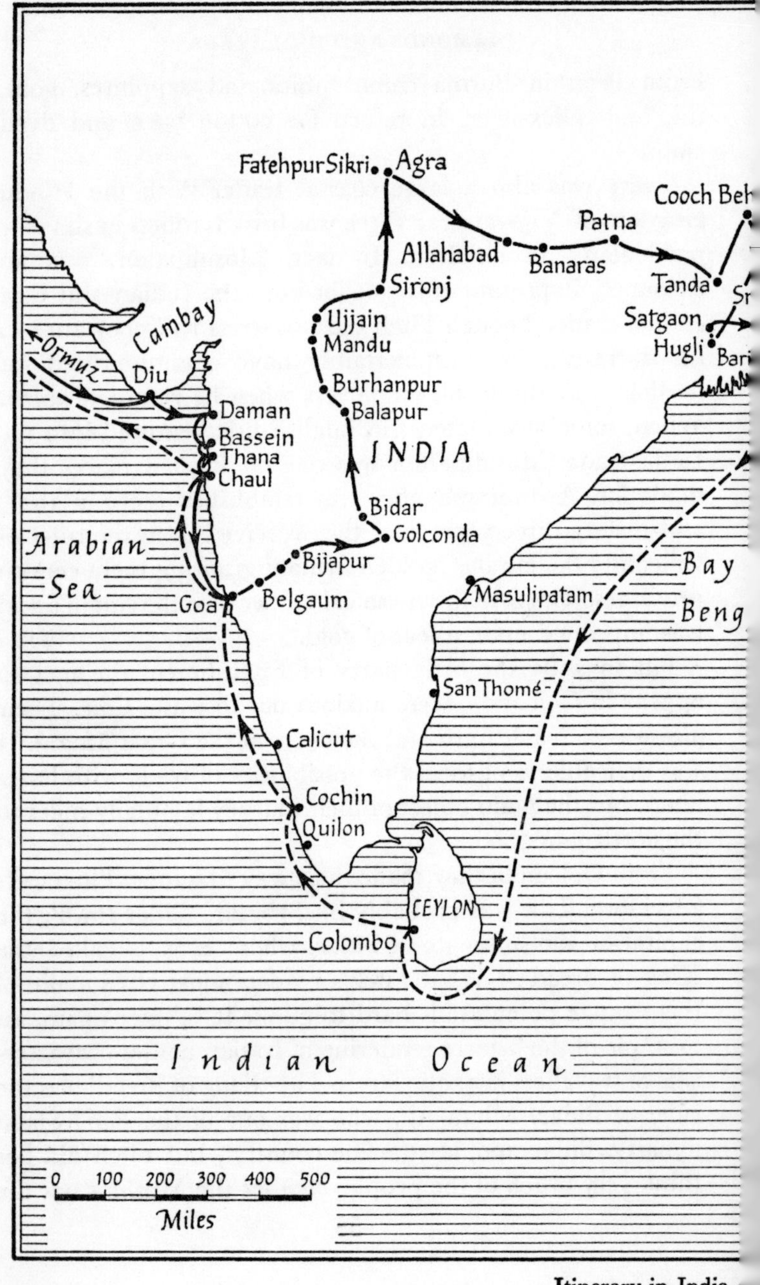

Itinerary in India

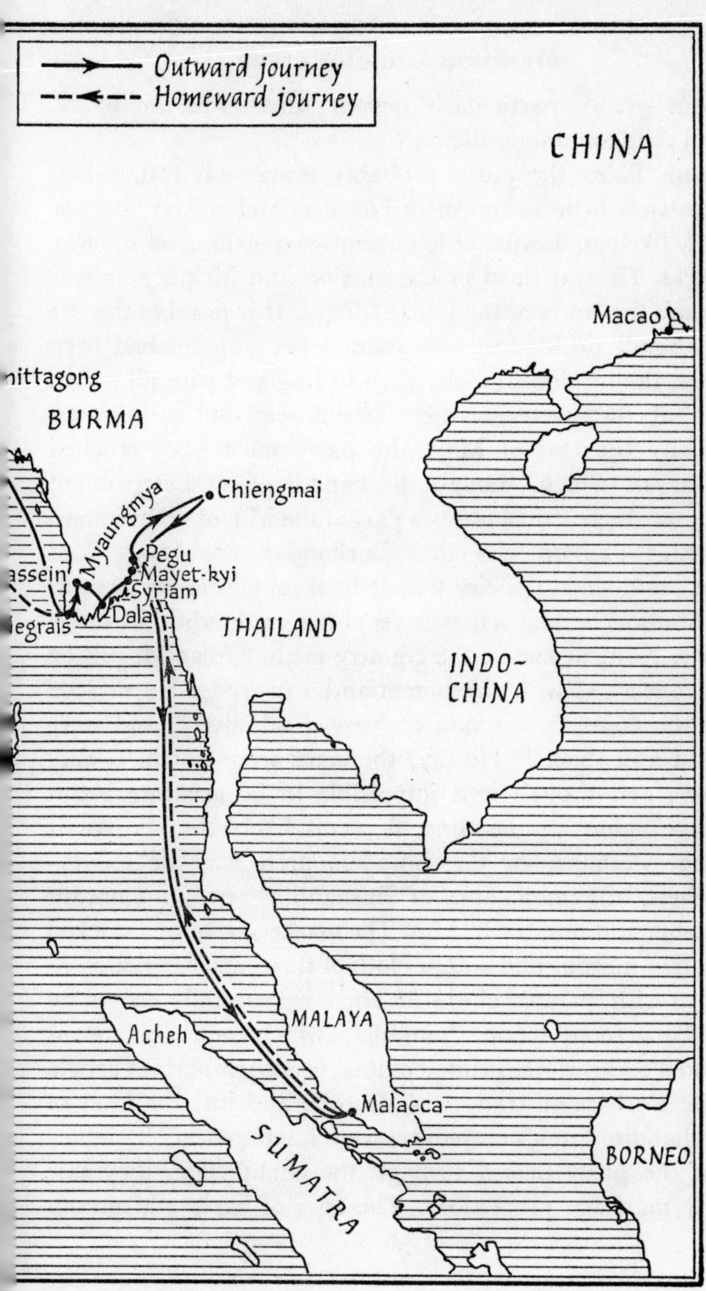

her Asia, 1583/90

Hindus seemed particularly devout; there was, he wrote, 'small religion among them'.[21]

From Bidar the party probably moved on rather fast. From what little is known of Newbery's character, he was hardly likely to dawdle or to encourage dawdling on the way to Agra. He was head of the mission and his purpose was to reach the court of the Great Mogul. It is possible that he had already decided that, as soon as the emperor had been visited, the mission should return to England with all speed. After all, they were not there as sightseers but as businessmen. By the end of May, the party must have reached Burhanpur which, though the capital of an independent state, was in practical terms a part of the Mogul's dominions.

Fitch's opinion was that Burhanpur was 'marvellous great', and since the city was at least four times as large as the London he had left two years before, he did not exaggerate. Now, at last in the country of the Great Mogul, he was concerned with the potentialities of trade. He noticed that the coins were made of 'very good silver', and were 'round and thick'.[22] He says the coins were worth 'twenty pence', and though it is impossible to be accurate about relative values at the time, it seems likely that he got it wrong. Perhaps, in the time-honoured way of money-changers, the merchants of Burhanpur saw an ignorant customer and profited by him. The markets were well stocked with fine muslins and cotton cloth of the coarser varieties, as well as with 'painted cloths'.[23] These were usually known by the Portuguese name, 'pintado', which actually means 'spotted'. This cloth, printed chintz, was an important article of the Portuguese trade with Europe and just the kind of merchandise Fitch's employers were interested in.

As the party passed through the countryside, they saw many marriage processions. The ages of bride and groom were surprising to the Englishmen—'boys of eight or ten years and girls of five or six years'.[24] The bride and groom 'both do ride upon one horse, very trimly decked, and are carried through the town to great piping and playing, and so return home and eat of a Banquet made of rice and fruits'.[25] But, Fitch added, 'they lie not together until they be ten years old'.[26] He must have asked the reason for such early marriages. 'They say they marry their children so young because it is an order that when a man dieth the woman must be burned with him; so that if the father die yet they may have a father-in-law to help bring up the children which be married; and also that they will not leave their sons without wives nor daughters without husbands.'[27] It seems that Fitch's informants tried to explain to him the nature and responsibilities of the Hindu joint family—and failed. But he certainly knew about the practice of widow-burning, or suttee. He had perhaps first heard of it during the journey to Goa, for he mentions that, in Cambay, 'when a husband dieth his wife is burned with him, if she be alive; if she will not her head be shaven and then is never any account made of her after'.[28] Usually, a widow was not given any option but to burn. By the time Fitch visited India, the practice—mainly confined to the upper castes—had become a solemn and religious obligation. The duty of a Hindu wife was to serve her husband in life and in death.

The Great Mogul himself, the emperor Akbar, did not approve of a widow being burned against her will, though he seems to have considered a voluntary act of self-immolation as something to be respected. Father Monserrate claimed that the emperor once insisted that the Jesuits witness a suttee, though this seems highly unlikely. Aquaviva is said personally to have reprimanded Akbar for 'showing openly by his presence there that he approved of such a revolting crime'.[29] A suttee could indeed be revolting, if the widow were unwilling. Monserrate writes—and he is supported by less biassed evidence—that the women were often drugged with opium and were not really aware of what was happening. Sometimes, he goes on, 'they are half-drugged; and before they lose their resolution are hurried to the pyre... On arriving they cast themselves into the flame. If they hesitate the wretched creatures are driven on to the pyre; and if they leap off again, are held down with poles and hooks.'[30]

Akbar's refusal to permit an unwilling woman to be burnt was given a dramatic underlining by his own interference in the obsequies of one of his Hindu nobles. The young man's family insisted that his widow should be burnt on her husband's pyre. She refused. But her son and his relatives were adamant. Akbar heard of the affair one morning while in the female apartments of his palace and immediately rode off unescorted to the spot where the pyre had been erected, pursued by a small bodyguard. He arrived alone, just in time to stop the ceremony. At first he was so angry that he proposed to execute those who had tried to force the woman on to the pyre, but later relented and merely imprisoned them for a short period.

The English travellers moved on from Burhanpur to the great city of Mandu, which Fitch records was 'besieged twelve years' by Akbar 'before he could win it'.[31] In fact, the siege was only of a few months' duration, though perhaps the sight of the fortifications made Fitch think they were almost impregnable. Mandu—the name means 'city of joy'—stands on the top of a hill and covers about eight square miles. The whole was formerly surrounded by a massive wall. Inside, there was a constant supply of water from wells and reservoirs. At the time of Fitch's visit, much of the city had fallen into ruins, but there were still enough buildings to indicate its magnificent past. There was a superb palace. with enormously thick walls relieved by deep-hewn arches. Inside, in the great hall of audience, the walls sloped inwards at such an extreme angle that the whole solid mass seemed to sway, so earning it the name of the 'swinging palace'.

The palace was the seat of the Mogul governor, and it is unlikely that the Englishmen would have seen the inside. But they could hardly miss the magnificent tomb of the city's founder, Hoshang Shah, with its glistening white marble, bright mosaics and inlay work, so beautiful a structure, in fact, that many years later Shah Jahan was to send his architects to it for inspiration in designing the Taj Mahal. The great mosque, too, was an impressive building, but the fame of Mandu had spread across India not because of its magnificence but because of the fidelity of a queen.

In 1560, when Akbar was consolidating his rule and expanding his empire, the kingdom of Malwa—of which Mandu was the capital—was an independent state ruled by Baz Bahadur. This ruler had begun his reign by murdering his younger brother and many of his nobles. In an age when military prowess was the first qualification for survival, Baz Bahadur was more interested in wine, women and music. Such an aesthete was obviously ripe for conquest. One of Akbar's generals, Adham Khan, was deputed to take Malwa, and in 1561 defeated Baz Bahadur in battle. As was the usual practice with Hindu rulers, Baz Bahadur had given orders that, should he be defeated, his wives and concubines who had been left in the fortress at Mandu were to be killed by men specially deputed to the task. His favourite wife was named Rupmati, and was 'renowned throughout the world for her beauty and charm'. When news of the defeat reached Mandu, Rupmati was stabbed with the rest of the women, but not killed. Adham Khan, who knew of her reputation, wanted her for himself. But while the conqueror was at the gates, the wounded Rupmati took poison and died. Her story caught the imagination. The love of Rupmati and Baz Bahadur was extolled in verse and painting, transforming the sordid horror of the event into the stuff of fairytale.

The city of Ujjain, to which Fitch, Newbery and Leedes next made their way, was the old capital of Malwa, It was a place of great antiquity and one of the seven sacred cities of the Hindus. Though much of its greatness lay in ruins, it was still important for Hindu astronomers, for it was the Indian Greenwich from which longitudes were reckoned. Fitch, however, as befitted a merchant, was more interested in their next stopping place, Sironj, for there was a 'great trade of cotton and cloth made of cotton, and a great store of drugs' there.[32]

Sironj was, in fact, famous for its fine chintzes. Other travellers had found that it was infamous for its unhealthy climate. Monserrate, who had passed through the town some ten years before Fitch, seems to have suffered from a plague of scorpions there. He also mentions a particularly unpleasant kind of lizard, whose 'bite was fatal . . . at least so the inhabitants of that region stoutly declare'.[33] On the whole, Monserrate found the town most unpleasant. 'Many of the inferior classes', he wrote, 'live in small round huts. Indeed, nowhere else in that region are such miserable hovels to be seen! The people live by agriculture, though the land that can be worked is scanty and poor. Their fields are everywhere surrounded by rocky hills, from which I suppose come the swarms of noxious beasts and especially of scorpions.'[34]

Fitch either did not notice the 'noxious beasts' or was more inured to them than the Jesuit father. But he does mention that at Sironj his party caught up with one of the Great Mogul's ambassadors on the march, 'with a marvellous great company of men, elephants and camels'.[35] This might well have been the cortège of Abdullah Khan, who had been sent to Goa with Monserrate with the intention of sailing for Europe and the court of Philip II of Spain. If it was, then history was displaying one of its neater coincidences. As a mission sent by Akbar in an attempt to reach the Western world arrived back, unsuccessful, three men from the West—disguised and probably on foot—were making their way to his court, emissaries of a queen of whom the emperor probably knew nothing, but whose bitterest enemy was that same king of Spain.

One thing was sure. The monsoon rains fell with equal severity on both parties. The difficulties of travelling in India in the rainy season were almost insurmountable. The countryside disappeared in a sea of mud; the main routes which were raised on embankments were usually passable, however, except when the rivers had risen more than usually high. During the monsoon most activities stopped—or, at least, those that required movement outside the towns and villages. It was the season of peace, for armies could not march, gunpowder would not ignite, and disease was rampant. The ambassador had his elephants which could wade across swollen rivers. Fitch and his companions had only their legs, and sometimes the rivers they had to cross were so deep and swift-running that they were forced to swim—'sometimes for our lives'.[36]

But the party pressed on. The rains at least would ensure that the Great Mogul was not away on some campaign on the distant frontiers of the empire. At last through the watery mist they could see the walls and towers, the mosques and domes, of the city of Agra. The long and troubled journey from the court of Queen Elizabeth to that of the Great Mogul was almost over—or so they thought.

V

The court of the Great Mogul

Fitch, Newbery and Leedes arrived at Agra some time in July 1585, only to find that the emperor and his court were at Fatehpur Sikri, twenty miles farther on. Naturally, the party wanted to reach the emperor as quickly as possible, especially as the rainy season was about to start in earnest and the roads would become even more difficult.

Whether Newbery had managed to conceal from the Portuguese Queen Elizabeth's letter to the emperor is not known. None of Newbery's later letters survive, and he did not live to write his own narrative. Fitch's reticence on the proceedings of the mission is therefore all the more frustrating. To his visit to the twin capital cities of one who was certainly the richest, and probably the most powerful, monarch in the world, Fitch gives only a few hundred words—and fails to record whether or not the party was received by Akbar.

Fitch's description of Agra—'a very great city and populous, built with stone, having fair and large streets'[1]—was unlikely to excite his readers, though he did go on to say, quite rightly, that it was 'much greater than London'.[2] As a city, however, London could at least claim to be older, for twenty years before the Englishmen's visit Agra had been little more than a village and a ruined brick fort, a place of little importance until Akbar's decision in 1565 to rebuild the fort in stone. According to Akbar's son and successor,

Jahangir, it took fifteen or sixteen years to build. To pay for the work, a special tax was imposed on the peasants. During his reign Akbar is said to have constructed 'five hundred buildings of masonry after the beautiful designs of Bengal and Gujarat which masterly sculptors and cunning artists of form have fashioned as architectural models'[3] inside the enclosure of the fort. Unfortunately, only a few survive today, as his grandson, Shah Jahan, destroyed most of them when he reconstructed the buildings in marble to suit his own taste.

At the time of Fitch's visit the buildings were of stone, like the walls of the fort itself, mostly of red sandstone. The fort stood on the bank of the river Jumna, and on that side there were pavilions with gilded windows and stone lattice work. Inside, the fort was more like a town than a military building. There were courts of law, places where the emperor held public and private audiences, baths, gardens with fountains and ponds. But when the emperor was away the courts and streets would be almost deserted, for the imperial following was really an immense caravan made up of thousands of people, soldiers, nobles, officials, servants and hangers-on of every kind, which moved from place to place as the emperor moved. So, too, did a vast army of tradesmen. The caravan that accompanied the emperor probably numbered more than 300,000 people as well as thousands of horses and elephants, menageries of exotic animals and birds. The imperial harem, too, numbered some five thousand women, three hundred of them for the emperor's pleasure, the rest servants and Amazon guards. Accompanying the harem were detachments of regular troops who escorted the women on the march and surrounded their quarters when they arrived at their destination. Literally thousands of the male retainers were employed in providing for the emperor's sport.

There were a thousand wrestlers and the same number of swordsmen; men who dealt with the mechanics of shooting and hunting; falconers for the hundreds of hawks; keepers of pigeons; and trainers of fighting animals from the largest and most ferocious down to frogs and spiders. It was no wonder that the cities of India seemed crowded when the emperor was in residence, and deserted when he was not.

Without the crowds, Agra was not as impressive as it should have been for an imperial city. It had grown up haphazardly, without any regular plan. Fitch mentions 'fair and large streets'[4] but there were in fact very few such. Most of the streets were merely winding, dirty alleyways. There were many gardens and groves but these were mainly enclosed, the private parks of the nobles whose mansions were scattered over the city. The domestic architecture of the rich was designed mainly for maximum privacy; outwardly it appeared dull and plain, for there were no windows on the sides facing the street. From a distance the city looked attractive, but once inside there was very little to see but blank walls. As for the common people, they lived in hovels and huts. One contemporary European observer remarked: 'To have seen one city is to have seen all.'[5] There was, however, one outstanding exception—the palace city of Fatehpur Sikri.

The road from Agra to Fatehpur was always full of people, servants of the court, great nobles on their way to the emperor surrounded by their escorts of brightly dressed horsemen, merchants from all over India, from Persia and China, all anxious to sell their wares, silk and rubies, diamonds and pearls, the exotic merchandise of the whole of Asia. Fitch noticed that some of the travellers rode in 'fine carts . . . and many of them carved and gilded with gold—with two wheels which can be drawn by two little Bulls

. The ramparts of Bijapur. Detail from a seventeenth-century painting showing
urangzeb at the siege of Bijapur. *Rampur State Library*, East Punjab.

6. Woman worshipping an 'idol' (*lingam*) at a Shiva shrine. Painting, c. 1550, from Mandu. *Victoria and Albert Museum*, London.

7. European view of a suttee. From Jan Huygen van Linschoten *Histoire de la Navigation* (Amsterdam 1638).

8. The queen of Golconda gathering diamonds, a fourteenth-century view. From the French illuminated manuscript known as the 'Livre des Merveilles'. *Bibliothèque Nationale*, Paris.

about the bigness of our great dogs in England'. Because of the amount of traffic along the road, there had grown up an almost continuous line of stalls and rest houses, 'as full as though a man was still in town'.[6]

The entrance to Fatehpur from the Agra road was, not unnaturally, through the Agra Gate, which led into the bazaar and then on to the main buildings of the palace city. Fitch's comments are confined to a line or two about the markets, and the remark that the town was 'greater than Agra, but the houses and streets be not so fair'[7]—a curious statement, acceptable only if Fitch was referring, as he must have been, to the business streets of the city. He makes no mention of the palace area, which he must have entered in the hope of an audience with the emperor, or of the history of the city.

That story had begun barely sixteen years before the Englishmen's visit. Akbar was without a male heir. He had made many pilgrimages to holy shrines and had offered many prayers for a son, without success. Then a Muslim holy man, Salim Chisti, who lived at Sikri, prophesied that the emperor's prayers would soon be answered. Early in 1569 one of Akbar's wives was reported pregnant and, in order to ensure maximum support from the holy man who had made the prophecy, was sent to Sikri to await the birth. In August, a son—later to be the emperor Jahangir—was born. In honour of the holy man and the efficacy of his prayers, the boy was given the name of Salim. Akbar also decided upon a more spectacular monument, the conversion of the obscure village of stone-cutters at Sikri into a great city. There were further sound reasons—or so the emperor believed—for the construction of a new capital. With the aid of his astrologers, the emperor had come to the conclusion that Agra was an unlucky city.

It was said that when the work of building the fort at

Agra had been completed the emperor 'found (for such was God's good pleasure) the place overrun with ghosts, which rushed to and fro, tore everything to pieces, terrified women and children, threw stones, and finally began to hurt everyone there'.[8] Even this might have been tolerated—for the astrologers would certainly have taken counter-measures —but 'the cruel spite of the Evil One began to wreak itself on the children of the King.'[9] Akbar's twin sons, Hassan and Hussain, who were born in 1564, had lived only a month. Like most of his contemporaries, Akbar recognised the reality of the occult. Sikri, with its lucky connotations—a holy man whose prophecies came true, the birthplace of a long-awaited heir—was surely a better place.

Building began in earnest in 1571 and continued in a whirl of activity, supervised whenever possible by the emperor himself. Most of the principal buildings were finished within nine years. The speed with which some of them were constructed demonstrates what drive and energy Akbar put into his project. Abul Fazl, the emperor's friend and the historian of his reign, did not exaggerate when he wrote: 'His Majesty plans splendid edifices, and dresses the work of his mind in stone and clay.'[10] Under pressure from the emperor, one building—a hall some two hundred feet long—was erected in three months, and a great line of baths with all their fittings was completed in six.

All this took a great deal of organisation. Akbar had even considered the question of noise. The shaped stone and cut timber 'he had . . . cleverly fashioned elsewhere in accordance with the exact plan of the building, and then brought to the spot, and there fitted and fastened together'.[11] A Jesuit visitor was 'reminded of what is said to have happened at the building of the temple of Jerusalem, when no iron instruments of the builders were heard', and 'saw that this could have been true without the intervention of a miracle'.[12] Akbar himself took part in the work of construction, sometimes quarrying the stone with the other workmen, and built a workshop for himself near the palace.

Sculptors and painters, craftsmen skilled in the inlaying of marble into stone, flocked from all parts of India to the new city. The result was a magnificent and harmonious blending of many styles.

The city was built upon the ridges of stone which marked the landscape of the area. Access to the palace section was not by roads, but by broad terraces and courtyards. Inside, there were two halls of audience, one for public receptions and another for more intimate gatherings, discussions with ministers and the reception of important ambassadors or vassal princes.

Of the dwellings that of the emperor was, naturally, the largest and most impressive. There was another for his wives, and one for the imperial princes. There were also storehouses and magazines. The decoration was elegant and luxurious, the walls covered with painting, marble inlay, and glowing tiles. Most of the buildings had pigeon cotes—Akbar was a great pigeon fancier and some twenty thousand birds of ten varieties were kept at court. The pigeons were cared for by eunuchs and female slaves. 'Their evolutions are controlled at will, when they are flying, by means of certain signals, just as those of well trained soldiery are controlled by a competent general by means of bugles and drums.' The way the birds could be made to dance in the air, turn somersaults, and return to their perches, was 'little short of miraculous'. By the sound of a whistle, 'they are bidden to perch on the roof, to conceal themselves within their nesting places, or to dart out of them again; and they do everything just as they are told'.[13]

The city was partially enclosed by a substantial wall, though this was designed less as a defence than to satisfy custom. All cities had walls. In case of attack, the city was not intended to be held; the court could conveniently take themselves to Agra, where the fort was strong and strategically placed on the river Jumna. Fatehpur—the name, which means 'city of victory', was added after Akbar's successful campaign in Gujarat in 1573—was a ceremonial city, like Louis XIV's Versailles. Like Versailles, it is a monument to what an autocrat could produce with almost unlimited funds provided by a helpless peasantry.

Fatehpur, for all Akbar's belief in its luck, was not a particularly healthy place. There were also problems over providing water. To supply the city a great artificial lake was dug north of the ridge on which the palace stood. The lake, some six miles long by two wide, fed a complicated series of waterworks leading into the city. Near one of the banks there was an amphitheatre for polo matches and combats between elephants.

These elephant fights were popular both with the emperor and with the people. They were also inclined to be dangerous, as the great beasts were not easily controlled. In order to protect the emperor from an unexpected assault, use was made of the elephant's great fear of fire. When watching an elephant fight, Akbar was protected 'by a bodyguard of soldiers who carry . . . bombs filled with powdered sulphur. These bombs are lighted and thrown into the arena, where they explode loudly.'[14] Polo, too, was an enjoyable sport which Akbar himself played with great enthusiasm. He had invented a luminous ball, made of the wood of the *dhak* or *palas* tree which smouldered when ignited, so that the game could be played at night.

But these were cold-weather pleasures. In the hot season it

was usual for the imperial princes and their friends to erect tents on the banks of the lake to take advantage of the coolness of the water. One day, three years before Fitch's arrival in Fatehpur, a party was gathered there playing chess and other games when, without warning, the embankment gave way. Though the torrent of water swept away houses below the ridge, drowning their inhabitants, the court party escaped unhurt. In thanksgiving, Akbar distributed alms and ordered that, on the anniversary day, no meat should be served at his table.

There were many stories Fitch and his companions could hardly have avoided hearing. They must certainly have enquired immediately whether there were any Portuguese in the city, for it was well known that the emperor had looked with considerable favour on some Jesuits from Goa who had spent some time at his court. They had arrived in 1580 at the personal invitation of the emperor, who had written to the Jesuits in Goa asking for 'two of your learned men, who should bring the books of the law, and above all Gospels, because I truly and earnestly desire to understand their perfection'.[15] The ambassador carrying Akbar's letter had been received with great ceremony at Goa. He was conducted from the ship that had brought him to the steps of the landing place where a great crowd of Portuguese gentlemen was waiting to welcome him. The ceremonial was very similar to that used to welcome a new viceroy. After his reception at the viceregal palace, a 'great train of cavaliers then accompanied him to our [Jesuit] College of St Paul where he presented to the Provincial the letters of his King'.[16] There was some hesitation on the viceroy's part about the wisdom of accepting the Great Mogul's invitation. It was possible that Akbar wished to lay hands on hostages to use against the Portuguese. But he left the decision to a council of bishops and they, at least, saw the possibilities.

An invitation of this kind from such a great monarch was an opportunity that could not be missed. The Portuguese remembered once again that they were in Asia not only to profit from Mammon, but to serve God. For years the Portuguese authorities had been searching for ways to introduce missionaries into the Mogul dominions. Now they were to be given access to the court, even to the emperor himself. The prospect of converting the emperor to Christianity opened vistas of both religious and political advantage.

The two men chosen, Fathers Aquaviva and Monserrate, had been more impressed than Ralph Fitch with the splendours of Fatehpur. They were also pleased with their reception by the emperor. The day after their arrival they were received in the Hall of Private Audience. Robed in black, with clean-shaven faces and tonsured hair, the fathers looked plain and austere among the great nobles, covered with jewels, dressed in fine coloured silks. The fathers presented the emperor with a copy of the famous polyglot Bible printed by the great printer, Plantin, for Philip II of Spain. The emperor paid the book great respect, kissing it devoutly. The fathers were allowed to prepare a room in the palace as a chapel, and Akbar's second son, Murad, was handed over to Monserrate for instruction in the Portuguese language and Christian morals.

Everything seemed to be going well. The emperor was impressed by the saintliness of Aquaviva and the aggressive faith of Monserrate who, in disputes with Muslim theologians, was particularly outspoken. But the Jesuits did not understand the emperor's mind. Dissatisfied with the faith into which he had been born, he was anxious to examine and be instructed on all the other faiths. As part of his policy he wished to show tolerance to all, but he was not prepared to commit himself to any single one, not even the faith of the élite of the empire.

In fact, Akbar was anxious to use the fathers as part of what turned out to be a deliberate attempt to lower the prestige of Islam in India and, in particular, to weaken the influence of Muslim theologians who disapproved of his free-thinking ways. On one occasion the emperor devised an essentially childish plan for disposing of one man who professed great sanctity. The suggestion was made, probably by an *agent provocateur* of the emperor, that the relative virtues of the Bible and the Koran—and of their supporters—should be tested by an ordeal of fire. One of the Muslims carrying a copy of the Koran, and one of the Christians carrying a copy of their holy book, would walk through a fire. The book that came out unharmed would be considered true. Father Aquaviva replied that his faith needed no miracles to demonstrate its truth, but later privately informed Akbar that he was quite willing to go through the ordeal. Akbar explained that he need have no fear of the flames. All the emperor wanted was the Jesuits' help in punishing a certain theologian who boasted that he was a holy man but was actually 'befouled with many and great crimes'.[17] Father Aquaviva would not be forced to go through the ordeal, only to say in public that he was willing. Akbar obviously anticipated that the 'holy man' could be persuaded to go through the fire first, and that no miracle would intervene to protect him. But Aquaviva would not agree, and the project was dropped.

Akbar's treatment of the Jesuits was undoubtedly designed to be provocative to others, but his tactics endangered the emperor's own position. Certainly, his attitude towards the Jesuits raised the distinct possibility of a plot against his life. For a while, the fathers thought that the emperor's deliberate hostility towards the Muslim faith was an indication of his imminent conversion to theirs. They wrote letters to Goa virtually announcing it. But they slowly came to realise that there was no real hope of bringing Akbar either into their religion or into alliance with Portugal.

In 1582, Monserrate quitted the court, ostensibly to take part in an embassy from Akbar to the king of Spain, though the ambassador never left India. Aquaviva stayed on, only to leave, sorrowfully, early in 1583. In July of that year he was murdered at Goa by a Hindu mob outraged by the priests' destruction of their temples. Fitch and his companions could have heard his story during their enforced stay in Goa. Certainly, Story must have done so, for it was from the Jesuit college of St Paul that the two fathers had left on their mission.

Perhaps, during their stay at Fatehpur, the Englishmen also heard of the new faith Akbar had invented for himself. Fitch, as a highly observant man anxious to learn as much about the country as he could, would soon have learned that the emperor had made many enemies among the orthodox Muslims, that not only had he openly rejected Islam but openly begun to persecute it. Akbar's new faith was supposed to be an amalgam of all, a supreme tolerance—but a stream of regulations was issued, most of them hostile to Islamic custom.

One regulation prohibited giving the name of Muhammad to children. New mosques were not to be built, nor old ones repaired. The slaughter of cows—particularly repulsive to Hindus, but not to Muslims, who ate beef—was forbidden in another regulation. Those who disobeyed were to be punished, even with death. Naturally, the regulations were resented. Naturally, there were tensions, intrigues, even conspiracies against the emperor, only inflamed by his blatant favour to the Jesuits. The conspirators looked for a rival to support, and one of more orthodox persuasion.

For some time, a threat to Akbar's throne had existed in the person of his younger brother, Muhammad Hakim, governor of Kabul. But an attempted rebellion was crushed in 1581, and in the same month in which Fitch arrived at Fatehpur, Muhammad Hakim died in Kabul at the age of thirty-one from chronic alcoholism. When the news reached Fatehpur, Akbar decided to leave for Kabul in order to consolidate his hold over the area.

This decision can have given Fitch and Newbery little time to ask for an audience, but it is unlikely that they would have allowed the emperor to depart without at least making an attempt to approach him. All Fitch will admit is that he saw the emperor dressed in a white tunic, 'made like a shirt, tied with strings on the one side, and a little cloth on his head coloured oftentimes with red or yellow'.[18] He might have added that Akbar, then in his forty-third year, was a strongly built man about five feet seven inches tall. When walking, he slightly dragged his left leg, though he was not lame. His complexion was rather dark, his face clean-shaven except for a small moustache. His eyes, according to Monserrate, were 'vibrant like the sea in sunshine', and he had a very loud voice of 'peculiar richness'.[19] The tunic mentioned by Fitch came down to the knee, and underneath he wore close-fitting trousers of fine silk tissue. In private, the emperor liked to dress in European clothes, and often wore a Portuguese suit of black silk or velvet. He never moved without a dagger at his waist or a sword near to hand —a wise precaution, considering the number of his enemies.

Perhaps Akbar's most interesting characteristic was that he was, at least formally, illiterate. Though he could neither read nor write, he had a phenomenal memory. He had books of history, philosophy and poetry read to him and could repeat most of what he heard. His curiosity about things and ideas was almost insatiable.

Fitch and Newbery would have had no difficulty in approaching him, for foreigners of every sort were welcomed at his court. Each day, Akbar would sit in the Hall of Public Audience and people of any rank could approach him. Before dawn people would gather to await the arrival of the emperor. Soon after the bright Indian sun had risen to create great areas of sharp shadow among the red stone pillars, Akbar would appear. Sometimes he would sit crosslegged on a mass of cushions or on a costly throne. Usually he preferred to stand at a window opening on to the audience hall. The hall would be crowded. On the roof, peacocks would be displaying themselves; elephants would be slowly exercised in the courtyard; and perhaps a groom would pass leading a hunting cheetah on a thick chain.

With the great, Akbar was stern and rigorously formal, but with the ordinary petitioner he was always kindly and sympathetic. Petitions were presented by a special officer. Orders were passed at once, so that there was no delay. Everything that was said was carefully recorded by a scribe. The emperor also held a second audience, but to this only the nobles, ministers and distinguished visitors were allowed.

There were, of course, other times when the common people could have a view of the emperor. Apart from the occasions of displays and animal fights, there were great festivals in which the emperor was the leading figure. One such was the festival of the New Year.

This ceremony was always a splendid one, but the Jesuits had had the privilege of witnessing a particularly lavish version in 1582 when Akbar chose to celebrate his victory over his brother, Muhammad Hakim. On this occasion, all the walls of the palaces were decorated with cloth of gold and silver tissue. Akbar himself was gorgeously dressed, and from a high throne of gold and precious stones distributed gifts to his victorious generals while all classes were treated to free food and wine and given a distribution of cash. Parts of the private apartments were opened to the public. Women were permitted to view the imperial zenana. There were games and other entertainments every day. One bizarre episode pleased the Jesuits. According to Monserrate, a relative of the emperor placed a picture of the Virgin Mary in the window in the audience hall at which Akbar appeared before his subjects, draping the picture 'with the most beautiful hangings of cloth of gold and embroidered linen'. Monserrate records that Akbar was pleased with the idea, and rather naïvely maintains that even the Muslim divines did not object when they 'perceived that non-Christians were worshipping and reverencing the picture and—as if compelled by the unaided force of truth—were not denying adoration to the image of her whom the morning stars extol, and whose beauty amazes the Sun and Moon'.[20]

Though there is no doubt that Akbar enjoyed the display of wealth and power—and loved the flattery that went with it—his real pleasure was in the hunt. Nothing seemed to affect his tremendous energy, not even the immense amount of wine (usually laced with opium) which he consumed. Sometimes the opium seemed only to enhance his natural daring and bravery, which were notable enough under normal circumstances. He was afraid of nothing. At the age of fourteen, he decided to mount an elephant named Hawai, meaning 'like the wind', which was notorious for 'choler, passionateness, fierceness and wickedness'. Finding the experience, in fact, rather dull, Akbar set Hawai to fight another elephant, equally vicious and bad tempered. But the other elephant fled, pursued by Hawai—with Akbar hanging on. The two elephants plunged down the steep bank leading to the river Jumna and raced across the bridge of boats which spanned it. Though they almost sank the pontoons with their great feet, both managed to reach the other bank and Akbar was at last able to bring Hawai under control.

Akbar's greatest passion, however, was war and the expansion of his dominions. His rule was essentially military, and his government an armed camp. Fitch and Newbery must have seen him depart in August 1585, intent on securing the possession of Kabul after the death of his brother and making a new conquest, that of Kashmir.

The emperor's military train was only slightly less ostentatious than his caravan on more peaceful occasions. The imperial harem was not quite so large, and the women chosen to accompany him would be carried on she-elephants, shut up in decorated cages. The female servants rode on camels, shaded by white umbrellas. The whole was surrounded by a guard of five hundred men. The imperial treasure, protected by a strong guard, was also carried on elephants and camels, while the baggage and ammunition went in two-wheeled carts. The camp furniture was transported on the backs of mules.

The force assembled outside Fatehpur was made up of fighting elephants, their great bulk protected by leather armour, on one flank; and mounted archers, pike men, and infantry on the other. The imperial party occupied the centre, with the artillery close by. When the force moved off, the emperor was preceded by drummers and trumpeters mounted on elephants. 'All . . . silent except one, who sounds his drum at short intervals . . . with a slow and dignified rhythm.'[21] Mounted scouts rode ahead to drive people away from the line of march.

Fatehpur must have seemed very tame after the emperor's departure. But no one could have known that he would return to the city only once again, for a short time thirteen years later. The great palaces of this wonderful city were to fall into decay, abandoned for some reason still unknown.

As for the three Englishmen, when the emperor left it was almost time for them to leave too. It was time, rather, for Newbery and Fitch to leave. Leedes, it appears, had managed to find employment at court. Fitch says that Leedes stayed at Fatehpur, and that the emperor gave him a 'house and five slaves, an horse, and every day six shillings in money'.[22] What happened to Leedes afterwards is not known; nothing further is heard of him.

Newbery left on 28 September 1585. He was to make for home by way of Lahore, 'determined from thence to go for Persia and then for Aleppo or Constantinople', [23] and on by ship to England. Newbery, as head of the mission, directed Fitch 'to go for Bengala and for Pegu and did promise me, if it pleased God, to meet with me in Bengala within two years with a ship out of England'.[24] But God did not please. Newbery never reached England, and nothing is known of what happened to him.

VI

A rich and prosperous country

Now on his own, Fitch left Fatehpur Sikri to make a leisurely journey across India to Bengal, from where he hoped to take a ship for Burma and farther east. Returning to Agra, he there joined a convoy of boats going down the river Jumna to the ancient city of Prayag, recently renamed by Akbar as Allahabad, 'city of God'. In the convoy were 180 boats, 'laden with Salt, Opium, Hinge [asafoetida], Lead, Carpets and divers other commodities'.[1] The river was an important highway for trade from north-western India to the east. Salt, a valuable commodity in a tropical country, came from the great lake of Sambhur in the Rajputana and from the salt mines of the Punjab. The opium poppy was widely grown, but some qualities were preferred by connoisseurs above all others. The carpets may well have come from the manufactories set up by Akbar at Agra and Fatehpur, but they were not a match for the fine carpets of Persia which passed through the markets at Agra. Asafoetida, a particularly strong-smelling gum resin, was used to flavour food but also, in small quantities, in a number of medicines.

At Allahabad, the Jumna joins and merges with the Ganges and, in Hindu mythology, with the sacred river Saraswati. The city was of considerable strategic importance. In October 1583, Akbar, who arrived there by river, gave orders for the erection of a great fort which still stands today. The work was hurried on with Akbar's usual speed and must have been finished and in occupation when Fitch arrived. Under its old name of Prayag, which means 'city of sacrifice', Allahabad had been a centre of pilgrimage and nothing about that had been changed except the name. Fitch arrived too late to witness the great religious fair held at the meeting of the rivers every year in early spring. Thousands of pilgrims from all over India would converge on the site, erect makeshift huts, and prepare to take a ritual plunge in the waters. But he did notice that there were great numbers of Brahmin priests around.

'In these countries', he noted, 'they have many strange ceremonies.' The Brahmins would come to the riverside, the sacred cord—made of three threads, each of nine strands of twisted cotton—which is the mark of the highest caste among the Hindus, over their shoulder. There they 'lade up water with both their hands, and turn the string cord first with both their hands within, and then one arm after the other out. Though it be never so cold they will wash themselves in cold water or in warm.'[2] Fitch observed, or was told, that the Brahmins lived on rice, butter, milk and fruits, and 'eat no flesh nor kill anything'.[3] They 'pray in the water naked', and ate their food naked, and 'for their penance they lie flat upon the earth and rise up and turn themselves about thirty or forty times, and use to heave up their hands to the sun and to kiss the earth, with their arms and legs stretched along out, and their right leg always before the left'.[4]

Every morning the Brahmins marked their forehead 'with a kind of yellow gear which they grind'.[5] In the streets there were men who carried a 'box of yellow powder',[6] made up essentially of sandalwood coloured with saffron, with which the marks were made—the three bars of the trident of Shiva, for example—as an indication of which god a man worshipped. The wives of the Brahmins, too, would go down to the river, and 'there do wash themselves and then use their ceremonies and mark themselves in their foreheads . . . and so depart singing'.[7] When Brahmins met, they did so with the salutation: 'Ram Ram' (God, God). But for all their apparent piety and the fervour of their observances, Fitch did not approve of them. 'They be a kind of crafty people,' was his final comment, 'worse than the Jews.'[8]

Fitch approved even less of Hindu holy men, whom he insisted on calling 'beggars',[9] though he noted that the Indians 'call them Schesche'.[10] What this word was actually meant to represent is obscure. One suggestion is that it is a version of the Sanskrit word *shishya*, a disciple, though it seems more likely that it is the Hindustani word *shaikh*, which means a priest. It could even, by one of those wonderful Elizabethan transformations, be a variation on *yogi*, for that is certainly what Fitch saw. He was naked, 'his beard . . . very long, and with the hair of head he covered his privities. The nails of some of his fingers were two inches long, for he would cut nothing from him, neither would he speak.'[11] The man had with him a number of disciples or hangers-on, who 'spake for him. When any man spake to him he would lay his hand upon his breast and bow, himself would not speak. He would not speak to the King.'[12]

Ordinary people were perhaps not quite so exotic, but they were unusual enough in appearance for it to be mentioned. 'The men for the most part have their faces shaven,' and their heads, too, 'except some which be shaven save the crown; and some of them are as though a man should set a dish on their heads and shave them round, all but the crown.'[13]

From Allahabad, Fitch continued down the river, this

time the Ganges, in the direction of Banaras. The river was very broad. 'Here is great store of fish of sundry sorts and of wild-fowl, as of swans, geese, cranes and many other things.'[14] The Ganges was broken by many islands and the water was 'very sweet and pleasant'.[15] The same could hardly be said for the river at Banaras, with its flotsam of partly burned bodies. Banaras was so sacred a place that many Hindus came to die there so that their ashes might be thrown into the Ganges, the sacred river of the god Shiva. Unfortunately, the pyres did not always consume the body completely, but it was thrown into the river anyway, and, wrote Fitch, 'dogs and foxes do presently eat them'.[16] Nor were the great wells or tanks inside the city itself free from pollution.

Fitch describes 'a great place made of stone, like to a well with steps to go down, wherein the water standeth very foul and stinketh'.[17] It is possible that Fitch was describing the artificial tank of the Manikarnika, which stands near the most important cremation spot. The tank is held to be very holy, for it is said to be filled with the sweat of the god Vishnu. The water is always full of decaying flowers, the tribute of worshippers who bathe in the water. 'There be always many people in it; for they say when they wash themselves in it that their sins be forgiven them, because God, as they say, did wash himself in this place.'[18]

All along the sides of the sacred river, steps run down to the water, crowded with bathers and worshippers. Some pray in the water, others 'wash a place which is their length, and they will pray upon the earth with their arms and legs at length out, and will rise up and lie down, and kiss the ground twenty or thirty time, but they will not stir their right foot'.[19] Others 'make their ceremonies with fifteen or sixteen pots, little and great, and ring a little bell, when they make their mixtures, ten or twelve times; and they make a circle of water round about their pots and pray'.[20] At another place on the river bank, Fitch observed a number of old men who 'gave the people three or four straws, which they take and hold . . . between their fingers when they wash themselves'.[21] Here he was probably referring to pieces of one of the many of India's sacred herbs. In return for this service and for the placing of a mark on their foreheads, the worshippers who 'have in a cloth a little rice, barley or money . . . when they have washed themselves'[22] give them to the old men, 'and when they give the old men say certain prayers and then is all holy'.[23]

Behind the bathing places were the temples, many hundreds of them, dedicated to all the gods of the Hindus. Inside, 'they have their images standing, which be evil favoured, made of stone and wood; some like lions, leopards and monkeys, some like men and women and peacocks, and some like the devil with four arms and four hands'.[24] One of the 'idols' which Fitch observed in a number of shrines was 'a kind of image which in their language they call Ada . . . This Ada hath four hands and claws.'[25] What he saw were probably images of the goddess Lakshmi, the consort of Vishnu, who is sometimes shown with four arms. Fitch's dislike of idolatry blinded his eye to the beauty of some of the images and deliberately exaggerated the repulsiveness of others. 'Many of them', he noted, 'are black and have claws of brass with long nails, and some ride upon peacocks and other fowls which be ill-favoured with long hawk's bills; and some like one thing and some another, but none with a good face.'[26] He saw, too, probably, images of the terrible black goddess Kali, the fierce and bloody consort of Shiva, with her necklace of skulls, 'their mouths monstrous, their ears gilded and full of jewels, their teeth and eyes of gold, silver, and glass'.[27]

In some of the shrines he saw men squatting by the side of the images, 'with a fan to blow wind upon them',[28] who when they saw a worshipper approaching rang a little bell to attract the attention of the god to the maker of an offering; 'many gave them alms', especially country people on a pilgrimage.[29] All the dark sanctuaries were lit with tiny lamps which were never allowed to go out, and no one was allowed into the shrine without first taking off his shoes. Fitch makes no comment on the perpetual noise of prayers and music, the clanging of bells and cymbals, the heavy smell of perfumed oil and incense, the sickly stink of millions of decaying marigolds and rose petals which made, and still make today, the climate of this sacred city. But he did, as always, notice the people.

Most he saw went 'naked save for a little cloth bound about their middle'.[30] The women had 'their necks, arms and ears decked with rings of silver, copper, tin and with round hoops made of Ivory, adorned with amber stones, and they are marked with a great spot of red in their foreheads'.[31] On one occasion, he seems to have watched a marriage ceremony by the waterside. As well as the man and woman and an old Brahmin priest, there were also a cow and a calf. 'Then the man and woman, cow and calf, and the old man, go into the water together, and they give the old man a white cloth of four yards long and a basket, cross-bound, with divers things in it.' The priest placed the cloth on the back of the cow, and 'then he taketh the cow by the end of the tail and sayeth certain words'. The man holds the priest's hand, and the woman the man's hand. The woman 'hath a copper or brass pot full of water . . . and they pour water out of the pot upon the cow's tail and it runneth through all their hands . . . then the old man doth tie him and her together by their clothes'. After this the couple walked round the cow and the calf and the marriage ceremony was over—except for the giving of alms. 'They give somewhat to the poor which always be there, and to the . . . priest they give the cow and the calf, and afterward go to divers of their idols and offer money and kiss it divers times, and then go their way.'[32]

Banaras must have impressed Fitch. For such an economical writer he was almost expansive. True to his commercial purpose, he mentioned that the city had also 'a great store of cloth, made there of cotton, and Shashes for the Moors'.[33] By 'shashes' he meant turban cloths, for which Banaras was famous. But of the real importance of the city as a place of pilgrimage, even of the gods who were worshipped there with such devotion, he seems to have learned little. He tells nothing of the rich intellectual life of Banaras, that 'Athens of India', as a later traveller was to call it.[34] Perhaps he did not stay in the city for long, as the merchants in the convoy of vessels with which he was travelling may well have finished their business and wanted to get on to the next port of call. Fitch does not say.

From Banaras, Fitch went to Patna, 'down the river Ganges, where in the way we passed many fair towns and a country very fruitful'.[35] He noticed the 'many very great rivers' that entered the Ganges, and was surprised when he saw that, of the partly burned bodies floating in the river, those of the men 'swim with their faces downwards, the women with their faces upwards'.[36] He thought that something must be tied to the bodies to produce this effect, 'but they say no'.[37] The living women 'be so decked with silver and copper that it is strange to see; they use no shoes by reason of the rings of silver and copper which they wear on their toes'.[38]

During the journey down river to Patna, Fitch seems to have come in contact with—or at least been told about—

bands of thieves who infested the countryside; remembering his experiences on the journey through Persia, he likened them to 'the Arabians, for they have no certain abode, but are sometime in one place and sometime another'.[39] Probably the merchants of the convoy told him of their own experiences. In fact, there were many tribes whose sole occupation was robbery. Naturally, with the river such an important highway for costly goods, these tribes were always ready to take advantage of any laxity among the guards during the night's stop.

Fitch, however, arrived at Patna—'a very long and great town'—without being robbed. He found the houses simple, but the streets 'very large'.[40] He also saw again one of those Hindu holy men whom he found so offensive. 'Here', he wrote, 'I saw a dissembling prophet, which sat upon an horse in the market place and made as though he slept; and many people came and touched his feet with their hands and then kissed their hands. They took him for a great man.' But Fitch did not—'sure he was a lazy lubber. I left him there sleeping. The people of these countries be much given to prating and dissembling hypocrites.'[41]

The trade of Patna was very considerable. There was the usual business in cotton and cotton cloth, but the town was also the centre of the sugar trade, for sugar cane was extensively cultivated in the area and was of particularly fine quality. Patna also exported to other parts of India 'very much opium'.[42] Cultivation of the opium poppy was encouraged by Akbar, and Patna opium had the reputation of being amongst the finest. There are no adequate statistics for either the production of raw opium or consumption of the processed version, but there is no doubt that, following the example of Akbar, the majority of nobles took opium in one form or another. The most popular seems to have been a spiced infusion known as *posta.* It does not seem to have been smoked at all, in fact.

The Jesuit father, Monserrate, while on his way to the court of Akbar, discovered at the town of Gwalior a sect of opium drinkers which had been founded by one Baba Kapur, some years earlier. Baba Kapur, 'a damnable fellow' according to Monserrate, believed that release from 'the ills of the flesh and the troubles of the mind' could be achieved through opium, and devised a 'poppy-pod drink'. Members of the sect—which, Monserrate was told, included Akbar—'eat no meat, onions, garlic, or anything of that kind. They even abstain from fruit and are particularly careful never to take any oil, which is fatal after opium or this drink.'[43]

On the whole, Fitch found the country rich and prosperous, the cities impressive, and trade extensive. From Patna he journeyed to the town of Tanda, which had once been the capital of Bengal before the Mughal conquest and was still an important place. But the tributary of the Ganges on which it stood was shifting its course, and within a hundred years of Fitch's visit Tanda had fallen into decay. In the jungles round about, the tiger roamed, and there was 'great store of wild fowl'.[44] The people were 'very great idolaters'.[45]

While he was at Tanda, it seems likely that Fitch heard that, to the north, there was a way to China. In his leisurely fashion he set off to find out for himself by visiting the independent kingdom of Cooch Behar, a journey of about 150 miles from Tanda. Again, Fitch's descriptions of what he saw are tantalisingly vague. He noted that the 'country is set with Bamboos', but seemed to think that it was near Cochin China, 'for they say they have pepper from thence'.[46] He reports that there was 'much silk and musk' and that the people 'have ears which be marvellous great . . . which they draw out in length by devices when they be young'.[47] There were 'hospitals for sheep, goats, dogs, cats, birds and for all living creatures; when they be old and lame they keep them until they die'.[48]

While in Cooch Behar, Fitch heard of a country four days' journey away called 'Botanter', whose 'King is called Dermain'. The country was Bhutan, and the king's name is presumably an attempt at *Dharma raja*. In Bhutan, Fitch was told, there were 'merchants which come out of China—and they say Muscovia and Tartary—and they come to buy musk . . . agates, silk, pepper and saffron like the saffron of Persia'.[49] Fitch was also told that there were 'very high mountains in this country, and one of them so steep that when a man is six days off he may see it perfectly'.[50] These were the Himalayas, and the steep mountain was probably Chumalhari in Tibet, which is nearly 24,000 feet high. The Himalayas, always the source and subject of legend, were described to Fitch as being so high that when the people there 'be upon the mountains they see ships in the sea sailing to and fro, but they know not from whence they come nor whither they go'.[51]

Fitch may have gleaned some of his misinformation from Tibetan merchants who regularly crossed into India with an important luxury product in considerable demand in the courts of India and south-east Asia. The Tibetans 'cut the tails of their kine and sell them very dear, for they be in great request and much esteemed in those parts'.[52] The Tibetans' 'kine' were yaks, whose bushy tails were made into the *chowrie*, or fly whisk, which was a traditional symbol of royalty. The 'northern merchants', as Fitch calls them, were dressed in 'woollen cloth and hats, white hosen . . . and boots'.[53] They had one characteristic he thought worth noting—they were 'very swift on foot'.[54] Fitch may in fact have seen Tibetans before his journey into Cooch Behar. In the winter, Tibetan merchants penetrated into the plains of northern India and Father Monserrate records coming across some of them at Kalanaur in the Punjab. His information is rather more picturesque than that of Fitch. The Tibetans, he said, never took off their clothes nor washed their hands, face or feet, because they thought it was 'sacrilege to befoul with dirt so clear and beautiful an element as water and one which when drunk quenches thirst'.[55]

From Cooch Behar Fitch took himself to the town of Hugli, 'which is the place the Portugals keep in the country of Bengala'. The journey there was made not by the most direct route, as that was 'full of thieves', but through the countryside, 'where we found but few villages, but almost all wilderness, and saw many . . . swine and deer, grass longer than a man, and very many Tigers'.[56]

It might seem odd, not to say foolhardy, for Fitch to pay an open visit to a Portuguese settlement of some importance after his experience at Goa. He would have expected the authorities at Goa to have circulated the names of the Englishmen who had fled, to all the settlements in India, after the receipt of King Philip's letter concerning them. Fitch, of course, was dressed as a native, and may have expected to escape detection that way, but it is reasonable to assume that he had made enquiries about Hugli before he entered it. If so, he would have learned that it was not really a part of Portuguese Asia; its governor was neither appointed by, nor took orders from the viceroy at Goa. Hugli was a product of private enterprise, and it naturally attracted soldiers of fortune and merchants, criminals and fugitives from other Portuguese settlements as well as priests and missionaries. The Portuguese at Hugli elected their own governor, and his job was to look after the interests of his constituents and no one else. An absconding Englishman would not have been given a second thought.

The Portuguese had been active in Bengal for at least forty years before its conquest by Akbar. Their ships brought costly silks, fine porcelains, and other luxury goods for sale and picked up cargoes of cloth and other commodities for resale elsewhere. For the most part, the Portuguese did not remain in Bengal after the trading season, but returned to Goa or to Malacca until the new season opened. Some of the goods imported by the Portuguese appeared at the Mogul court—perhaps in the normal way of trade, or as a deliberate consignment sent in the hope of attracting the custom of the emperor. In 1577 Akbar sent for the leading Portuguese merchant adventurer, Pedro Tavares. Naturally, such a business opportunity was welcomed with enthusiasm, and Tavares, with two other merchants and a large suite of servants, set off for Agra.

There he was received by the emperor, who seems to have taken an instant liking to him. Tavares promised to maintain a constant supply of luxury goods from China and elsewhere if the emperor would grant him a place in Bengal at which he could erect warehouses and where the Portuguese could take up permanent residence. Akbar agreed and also gave the Portuguese permission to build churches and follow their religion without interference. Better still, perhaps, Tavares obtained exemption from the payment of customs dues. This seems to have done no more than regularise the position as it stood, for the Portuguese had managed to avoid paying duties ever since their arrival in Bengal.

Tavares returned to Bengal either at the end of 1579 or the beginning of 1580, chose his site, and immediately began the erection of stores, houses and churches. By the time of Fitch's visit both the town and its trade had grown enormously, so much so that Mogul officials at the port of Satgaon complained to the emperor of a severe loss of revenue. Nature was also turning against the prosperity of Satgaon. The river on which this port stood was a tributary of the main river known, like the new Portuguese town, as the Hugli. The river was full of sandbanks, which were constantly shifting, and the channel to Satgaon began to silt up. It is possible that Tavares had noticed the change in the level of the river and deliberately sited his new settlement at a spot where the water was still deep and free from obstruction.

The Portuguese called Satgaon 'Porto Piqueno', or 'little port' to distinguish it from Chittagong, which was the 'Porto Grande', or 'great port'. Despite the silting up of the channel and the competition from the Portuguese at Hugli Satgaon remained an important trading centre with a market every day for the sale of rice and other commodities. These were moved by way of the river in large boats with 'twenty-four or twenty-six oars to row them'.[57] The same type of vessel was used to bring up more exotic merchandise off-loaded from sea-going vessels at the port of Hijli, which stood at the mouth of the river on the Bay of Bengal. To Hijli came vessels from Sumatra and Malacca, as well as from other parts of India.

The Venetian traveller, Cesar Federici, who had passed this way some years before Fitch, went up river from Hijli to Satgaon by one of the boats. As this was the most convenient way of travelling, Fitch probably did the same. Federici records that, even though the boats were very light and the oarsmen highly skilled, they could not move up the river when the tide was running, 'but for refuge must make them fast to thc bank of the river until the next flowing water'.[58] When the tide was in their favour, however, the oarsmen would make the journey of about a hundred miles in eighteen hours. Just below Satgaon was a place where the larger vessels halted because they could go no further. Every year the merchants and sailors made and unmade there 'a Village, with Houses and Shops made of straw, and with all things necessary to their uses'.[59] When the trading season was over and the sea-going ships about to leave, 'every man goeth to his plot of Houses and there setteth fire to them, which thing', commented Federici, 'made me to marvel. For as I passed up to Satgaon, I saw this Village standing with a great number of people, with an infinite number of Ships and Bazars, and at my return coming down with my Captain of the last Ship, for whom I tarried, I was all amazed to see such a place so soon razed and burnt, and nothing left but the sign of the burnt Houses.'[60]

At Hijli, Fitch saw a 'great store of cloth which is made of grass which they call Yerva'.[61] This part of India was famous for grass cloth, and Fitch's word 'yerva' is probably a mis-hearing of 'herba', the more common word used by foreign travellers. Cesar Federici mentions *panni d'erba*, cloth of herbs or grass. What plant was actually used is not known, but it was probably a variety of stingless nettle.

From Hijli, Fitch seems to have gone to the port of Chittagong, on the far side of the Bay, though as usual he is vague about how he got there. He may have gone by the land route through the state of Tipperah, but it is more likely that he used the network of waterways at the mouths of the Ganges. If he did, then he would certainly have passed the island of Saugur. He does not seem to have heard of what went on there once a year. At least, he does not mention it, and with his contempt for the heathen he would hardly have ignored this further example of the absolute darkness in which dwelt the pagan.

A traveller who witnessed the yearly festival at Saugur a

few years after Fitch had passed that way describes the arrival of great crowds of pilgrims from all over Bengal. In preparation, the pilgrims had their heads and beards shaved, then washed and anointed themselves with sweet-smelling oil. They entered the temple to the sound of music and the blowing of conch shells, which wailed like mournful trumpets. The sickly smell of incense and many flowers seems to have created a sense of exaltation, for the pilgrims begged the god to accept their lives as a sacrifice. Certain that their offering was accepted, the pilgrims with great cries of happiness ran down to the beach. Awaiting them would be a gathering of sharks. Still in their ecstasy, the men and women marched into the sea and the sharks rushed among them. 'Since they are accustomed and thus encouraged by constantly tasting human flesh, they become so bloodthirsty that they rush up fiercely even at a shadow.'[62]

But to this horror which so upset the European eye-witness was sometimes added another, more subtle, and in the view of the pilgrims much more horrible. Towards the end of the festival, the sharks—gorged with a surfeit of human flesh—would not bother with the offerings. They would laze on the surface of the water, nose an offered victim, and then reject him. For the pilgrim, this was as if God had rejected his sacrifice, and he would leave the water overcome with grief, alive in an emptiness to which God had consigned him.

Fitch has little to say about Chittagong except that there were almost continuous wars in the area between the rulers of Tipperah and the kings of Arakan. The Portuguese had been active at Chittagong for some fifty years, taking part in the various wars and suffering heavily on occasion. When Fitch made his visit, Chittagong was part of the kingdom of Arakan, a state whose people were Buddhist by faith. The town was a great centre of trade; Cesar Federici had noticed on his visit eighteen large ships in the harbour. Many of the ships on their way to Hugli called first at Chittagong. They carried from Malacca, Sumatra and Borneo all kinds of fancy cloth in every colour except black, which was considered unlucky in Bengal. From Malacca came cloves, nutmegs and mace, and from Borneo the much-prized camphor. Cinnamon was brought from Ceylon and pepper from Malabar, and from the islands of the Maldives quantities of tiny white sea shells then used extensively as a form of currency and known as cowries. There would be cargoes of both red and white sandalwood from Solor and Timor, expensive but much in demand; lacquerware and silks, gilt furniture, and porcelain from China.

But the Portuguese at Chittagong were not all ordinary merchants. There were pirates, too, and—worse—slave traders. The headquarters of that particular business were not at Chittagong itself, but at Dianga, which stood on the opposite side of the Karnaphuli river and was leased from the king of Arakan. The pirates and slavers of Dianga were a continuous thorn in the side of the more respectable Portuguese merchants of Chittagong and Hugli, and a perpetual menace to the diplomatic activities of the viceroy of Goa, since their depredations were always brought up as a synonym for Portuguese violence and general dishonesty. The pirates, in fact, terrorised the coasts of the Bay of Bengal, attacking the forces both of the Mogul governors of Bengal and the King of Arakan if they attempted to interfere in the trade.

The slavers would depart from Dianga in small, light half-galleys, called galleases, and sweep the coastal seas for unwary fishermen. They would then sail into the hundreds of waterways that make up the mouths of the Ganges, sometimes penetrating a hundred miles into the interior.

Without warning they would descend on helpless villages, 'carrying away the entire population ... on market days, and at times when the inhabitants were assembled for the celebration of a wedding, or some other festival'.[63] Their treatment of prisoners was cruel. They 'pierced the palms of their hands, passed thin slips of cane through the holes and shut them huddled together under the decks of their ships. Every morning they flung down some uncooked rice, as we do for fowl.'[64]

The slavers did not want old men or women, so they offered them for sale at the place where they had been captured. 'It was usual to see young persons, who had saved themselves by timely flight, endeavouring today to redeem the parent who had been made captive yesterday.'[65] The rest were taken off for sale to Portuguese settlements as far away as Goa and Malacca, or to the Arakanese who used them as workers in the rice fields. Those that were sold in Bengal, often to other and more respectable Portuguese, were usually taken to the port of Pipli at the mouth of one of the waterways of the Ganges delta, or further down the east coast of India to Palmyras Point in Orissa.

From Chittagong, Fitch went to Barisal on the river Tetulia, one of the many rivers that make up the mouths of the Ganges. He found the local ruler 'a man very well disposed ... His country is very great and fruitful and hath a store of rice, much cotton cloth and cloth of silk. The houses be very fair and high-builded, the streets large.'[66] Though both men and women appeared to wear few clothes, the latter had 'great store of silver hoops about their necks and arms, and their legs are ringed with silver and copper and rings made of elephants' teeth'.[67]

Fitch was now in an area which, though nominally conquered by Akbar, was in almost continuous revolt against the

Moguls. At Sripur on the river Padma, Fitch noted that everyone thereabouts was in rebellion against the Mogul, 'for here are so many rivers and islands that they flee from one to another, whereby horsemen cannot prevail against them'.[68] Some forty miles from Sripur was the capital of lower Bengal, the town of Sonargaon, whose ruler, Isa Khan, was one of the leaders of the resistance to the Mogul conquerors. Fitch reports that the 'best and finest cloth made of cotton that is in all India'[69] came from there. Isa Khan was 'a great friend to all Christians', especially, one would imagine, to the Portuguese who were responsible for much of the trade which, through customs dues and other profits, supplied some of his revenue. Many of the people Fitch considered 'very rich', though the majority of the houses were 'very little and covered with straw and have a few mats round about the walls to keep out dogs and foxes [jackals]'.[70]

At some time in November, Fitch returned to Sripur. There seems to have been an important Portuguese settlement in or near the town.

What Fitch's plans had been when he left Fatehpur Sikri after the departure of Newbery, he does not say. Obviously, the arrangement to meet Newbery and a ship from England in Bengal in two years' time could only have been tentative. In any case, there was still another year to go and Fitch was hardly the type to stand still when he had seen all he initially intended to see. At Sripur he must have had some contact with the Portuguese merchants and sailors. The information that a vessel was about to depart for Burma probably decided his next move for him. Whatever the explanation, on 28 November 1586 he boarded a small vessel belonging to one Alberto Carvalho and sailed down river and into the Bay of Bengal.

VII

Lord of the White Elephant

As the ship of Alberto Carvalho emerged from the river mouth and made for the coast of Arakan, it passed the island of Sandwip, famous for its salt, headed towards Chittagong, and then, with a fair wind, moved down towards a landfall at the port of Negrais some five hundred miles to the south. The tiny ship was very overcrowded, and it was lucky that the weather was kind, for 'if any contrary wind had come we had thrown many of our things overboard, for we were so pestered with people and goods that there was scant place to lie in.'[1] It was, in fact, the time of year when the winds gathered in the Bay and could sweep up the coast, flooding the low lying land with tidal waves as high as twenty feet.

On Negrais, Fitch makes no comment other than to say of the bay that it had a 'brave bar and hath four fathoms of water where it hath least'.[2] Yet the first sight the sailor would have of this port in a new land would have been the superb Hmawdin pagoda. Gasparo Balbi, a Venetian jeweller who made the journey a few years before Fitch, saw the sun glistening on the pagoda for a full day before making port. The pagoda was covered with gold leaf and, 'because the rain washeth it often and consumeth the gold, the men of that place often regild it, that the ships by the splendour thereof may have this benefit to know the Haven'.[3] Balbi also gave one important piece of information—Negrais was beset by 'continual winds that blow there with great fury'.[4] Again, Fitch seems to have been lucky.

From Negrais the ship went up river to a place Fitch calls Cosmin. This may have been present-day Bassein, but it is more likely to have been a town on the Myaungmya river, which, though a series of creeks, was the main water highway to Pegu. Whichever it was, Fitch found it a 'very pretty town . . . very well furnished with all things'.[5] The people were friendly, and their houses were built off the ground on posts, 'and they go up them with long ladders for fear of the tigers which be very many'.[6] This area of Burma is a flat alluvial plain, intersected by hundreds of waterways, 'very fruitful of all things . . . very great figs, oranges, cocoes [coconuts] and other fruits'.[7]

Naturally, the people went about their business in boats; Fitch calls them 'paroes', a word with a variety of spellings given to any small craft. More important people had more important vessels. The governor of 'Cosmin', according to Balbi, had a 'Barke made very fantastically'. It was narrow in the middle and quite long, and 'at the head and stern it was as narrow as our Gondolas'. It had 'an hundred Rowers' all pulling together to the notes of 'four Trumpeters, which sound when they should row'. The governor sat in a high cabin in the centre.[8]

At 'Cosmin' Fitch transferred from Carvalho's vessel to one of the paroes for the journey through the waterways to Pegu. At one town on the river there were hundreds of boats, all carrying people and goods, many of the people with a large umbrella 'to keep the sun from them, which is as broad as a cartwheel, made of the leaves of the coco trees and fig trees and is very light'.[9] Some of these boats were actually the homes of their owners and were partly roofed over. From them were sold 'fresh fish and salted and dressed in divers fashions, and other sorts of provisions', so that those using the river 'may sail without carrying any victuals, but only money to spend.'[10]

At another stopping place which cannot be accurately identified, Fitch found eighteen or twenty 'very great and long houses, where they tame and keep many elephants of the king's; for thereabout in the wilderness they catch the wild elephants'.[11] Elephants were an important military weapon. The King of Pegu was said to have four thousand fighting animals and many more for state ceremonial. The capture of wild elephants for the royal stables was a highly organised affair, in which the king and his courtiers would often take part for sport. The hunters used female elephants to lure the wild males, for 'without the she, they are not to be taken'.[12] Each of the hunters would have a squad of five or six females, and 'they say that they anoint the she-elephant with a certain ointment, which when the wild elephant doth smell he will not leave her'.[13]

With the huntsmen on the back of the she-elephants, and the wild males following, all was ready for the capture. A place would have been prepared and covered with trees and boughs so that it looked like a dark thicket. In fact, however, it was the entrance to a stockade, with a gate like a portcullis which could quickly be lowered. When the wild elephants were inside, the females were removed. 'When the male seeth that he is left alone he weepeth and crieth and runneth against the walls, which be made of so strong trees that some of them do break their teeth [tusks] with running against them.'[14] The elephant was allowed to tire himself in this way and was then goaded with pointed sticks into a narrow building, and 'there they put a rope around his middle and about his feet and let him stand there three or four days without eating or drinking, and then they bring a female to him, with meat and drink, and within few days he becometh tame'.[15]

Neither Fitch nor other contemporary western travellers tell us anything of the training of war elephants. Fitch notes that, when prepared for action, 'they set a frame of wood upon their backs, bound with great cords, wherein sit four or six men, which fight with guns, bows and arrows, darts and other weapons'.[16] Before a battle, the elephants were primed with a drink of spirits and must have been a terrifying sight to the enemy, trumpeting ferociously, some even brandishing a great sword in their trunk. They were trained to tear down obstacles and, above all, to kill. Sometimes they were given rewards which could only have inflamed their ferocity. On one occasion, after the siege and capture of a city, the founder of the kingdom which Ralph Fitch was now visiting ordered all the dead children to be chopped up very small, mixed with bran, rice and sweet herbs, and given to his war elephants to eat.

Elephants were also used in executions. Selected animals were specially trained to take their time over the operation. They would pick up the criminal in their trunk and hurl him about, then worry him with their great tusks, and finally crush him slowly under the weight of their great feet. But there were also elephants of even more value to the king, elephants who did not fight or maim or kill, but were instead magical symbols of power, talismans of such potency that terrible wars were fought over their possession. These animals were, of course, kept at the capital, and Fitch had still some distance to go before he reached there.

Still moving by water, Fitch arrived at a town on the river on which the capital stood. Here he disembarked, probably because of the difficulty of rowing against the strong downriver current. The town—Fitch calls it Macao which could mean Makhau—about twelve miles from Pegu, was obviously a normal disembarkation point for visitors to the capital. There, men were waiting with a contrivance known as a *deling*, a kind of hammock strung on a pole. The traveller got inside, a cushion was placed at his head, and four men lifted the pole. At a jog trot, they made the journey to Pegu in a few hours.

The dynasty which now held the throne of Pegu had exercised power for barely half a century, and there were many still who disputed its right to the throne. The kingdom had been founded by two remarkable men, Tabin Shwe-ti—a title meaning 'The Topmost Golden Parasol'—and the present king's father, Bayin-naung, another title meaning 'The King's Brother'. In 1535 these two set out to recreate the kingdom of Burma which, for three centuries after its fall to the armies of Kublai Khan, had been divided into four independent states. Before this, Burma had been ruled by a dynasty of the first of the four principal races inhabiting Burma, the Burmese, the Shans, the Talaings and the Arakanese, and in 1535 each had a separate kingdom. The Burmese Tabin Shwe-ti was the Lord of Toungoo, in the centre of the country. To the north and east were the Shans; the Arakanese occupied the western coastal strip; and the Talaings the south of the country. The Talaing capital was at Pegu, and the two Burmese entered it as conquerors in 1539.

But the Talaings were not yet defeated, still holding out in the town of Prome and in the great and wealthy port of Martaban. To help him capture the latter, Tabin Shwe-ti did what many another Asian prince was doing at the time. He hired a band of Portuguese mercenaries, seven hundred men with muskets and light artillery, as well as ships under the command of one Joao Caeiro. The Talaing viceroy of

Martaban had in his employ another contingent of Portuguese, commanded by a certain Paulo da Seixas. In spite of the fact that the Burmese king had an immense army and a large number of elephants, he was unable to take the city by storm. The Portuguese artillery was too light to have any effect on the fortifications, and the waterside was defended by Seixas and seven Portuguese ships.

The siege dragged on for seven months, and the inhabitants of Martaban were starving. The viceroy asked for terms and received only a demand for unconditional surrender. The viceroy's last hope lay with the Portuguese mercenaries on the Burmese side, for their commander had once been in his employ and had gone over to the Burmese only in response to that most convincing of mercenary orders—a better offer. He therefore sent Seixas, disguised as a Burmese, to Caeiro with a letter in which he offered not only to become a vassal of the king of Portugal but to give Caeiro half his treasure of gold and precious stones. Caeiro would have been inclined to accept, but many of his followers so disliked the thought of the honours that would be given to him by the king of Portugal that they threatened to denounce him to Tabin Shwe-ti.

With his last chance gone, the Talaing viceroy agreed to surrender on the promise of his life—which was given, but not kept. Martaban was sacked and sixty thousand people killed.

After Martaban, the Lord of Toungoo had himself crowned king of Burma and set off on an expedition to conquer Arakan. Again he had a force of Portuguese mercenaries with him, but this time he was forced to come to an agreement with the king of Arakan so that he might hurry back to the south, where the Siamese, taking advantage of his absence, had attacked Burmese territory at Tavoy.

Actually, Tabin Shwe-ti used this minor incursion as an excuse for extricating himself from the unsuccessful campaign in Arakan. Tabin Shwe-ti had always intended to attack Siam, for the king of that country possessed a number of white elephants which Tabin Shwe-ti coveted. But the Burmese king's attempt in 1548 to seize the Siamese capital of Ayuthia and the elephants that were kept there was a failure.

This seems to have broken Tabin Shwe-ti's morale. He took to drinking heavily, allegedly under the influence of a young Portuguese, and handed over affairs to others. During a rebellion he was murdered. Bayin-naung, with the help of Portuguese mercenaries, suppressed the revolt and had himself crowned king at Pegu in 1551. Having re-established the kingdom of Tabin Shwe-ti, he then began his own ever-widening conquests. He attacked Siam in 1563 and captured the city of Ayuthia, sending most of the royal family off to Burma as hostages. He also captured the king of Siam's white elephants, and they too were despatched to Pegu.

Unfortunately, while Bayin-naung was away in Siam, rebels had attacked and burned Pegu, destroying the new buildings, including the royal palace which Bayin-naung had erected. When he returned, Bayin-naung immediately began to rebuild on the most luxurious scale. It was this new and magnificent city that Fitch was now entering.

In fact, there were two cities, Fitch calls them the Old and the New. The Old was surrounded by a high wall of stone and by a substantial moat. The houses there were mainly of bamboo and matting, though the merchants had attached to their homes a warehouse built of brick—for wooden houses 'oftentimes . . . take fire and burn in an hour four or five hundred'.[17]

The trade of Burma came through the ports of Negrais,

Martaban and Syriam. To the first port came ships from Bengal, carrying mainly cotton cloth, the fine white muslins much in demand in farther Asia. Also cotton yarn dyed red, 'which will never lose his colour'.[18] Opium, too, was a principal commodity of trade. Some came from Bengal and some, with printed fabrics, from the Portuguese settlement of San Thomé on the coast of Coromandel, near what was later to be the town of Madras. Goods from China and the Spice Islands were landed at Martaban, and Syriam seems to have received woollens, 'velvet, opium, and suchlike'.[19]

At Pegu, foreign trade was carried on through eight official brokers who 'are bound to sell your goods at the price they be worth, and you give them for your labour two in the hundred' [i.e. two per cent].[20] By this method, the foreign merchant was assured of actually receiving the money for his goods, for the brokers were responsible for selling the goods *and* for seeing to it that the merchant was paid. 'If the broker pay you not . . . you may take him home and keep him at your house; which is a great shame for him.'[21] In fact, the honesty of the brokers was widely acknowledged and appreciated by foreign merchants. Though Fitch does not mention it, the same could hardly be said for the officers at the Customs House.

Courtiers had a habit of taking their cut, usually by allowing their servants to steal from among the goods displayed in the Customs House for valuation. 'There come many gentlemen accompanied with a number of their slaves, and these gentlemen have no shame that their slaves rob strangers . . . they laugh at it! . . . Although the merchants help one another to keep watch and look to their goods, they cannot look thereto so narrowly but one or other will rob something.'[22]

Whether Fitch did any business himself he does not say.

It is not improbable the he had invested some of his money in goods loaded on to Alberto Carvalho's ship. As a merchant by profession, it seems unlikely that he would have been content merely to observe. He must have had contacts with the foreign merchants, of whom there were many in the Burmese capital. But, again, he does not say.

From the Old town Fitch entered the New. This too was surrounded by walls and a moat—a 'great ditch . . . with many crocodiles in it'.[23] There were no drawbridges across the moat, but permanent embankments leading to twenty gates, five in each side of the wall which was built in the shape of a square. At each of these gates there were watch-towers, made of wood 'gilded with gold very fair'.[24] Inside, the streets ran across the city from the gates, 'so broad that ten or twelve men may ride abreast through them'.[25] The houses that lined the streets were made of wood 'covered with tiles'[26] and at the front of each was planted a tree, so that there was 'a very fair show and a very commodious shadow so that a man may walk in the shade all day'.[27]

At the centre of the New city lay the king's palace with its associated buildings. For security, it was surrounded by yet another wall and a moat. Inside were a number of structures built of wood, 'very sumptuously gilded'.[28] On the roofs were many pinnacles, exquisitely carved, some gilded, some actually plated with thin sheets of gold, studded with semi-precious stones. The design of buildings in Burma was subject to very carefully regulated sumptuary laws. Only persons of a certain rank were entitled to live in a double-roofed house painted white. These laws also extended to many other aspects of life. Only the king himself and the White Elephant were entitled to white umbrellas. The crown prince and high dignitaries of state were permitted gold umbrellas, twelve to fifteen feet high, in numbers according to rank. Innumerable regulations covered such things as the size, shape and metal of spittoons, of buttons, of anklets. The cut and the material of clothes, their length, and the pattern woven into the cloth, all had precise hierarchical attributes. A man's rank and occupation could always be told by his dress when he was alive, and by the style of his funeral when he was dead.

The reasons for the special reverence paid to the White Elephant would have been impossible for Ralph Fitch to grasp, for they emerged from a world of fantasy to which he had no access. The Jesuits, when they came in contact with this world, saw it only as a facet of paganism, and the White Elephant either as a heathen god or as a devil. Fitch, in his down-to-earth way, observed only a pampered beast. But the kings of farther India saw a symbol, possession of which brought both spiritual and temporal power.

These kings were Buddhists and Buddhism, unlike Hinduism, has no place for kings and rulers; in fact, government of any kind was considered to be one of the Five Evils. But kings there were, and there had to be rituals and ceremonials in which they could demonstrate their kingship. Buddhist kings, therefore, took these from Hinduism. At Buddhist courts there were Brahmins whose duty it was to supervise such important ceremonies as the king's coronation and funeral, as well as those—such as the ploughing ceremony—which ensured the fertility of the land. The Hindu concept of kingship, which was of great antiquity, included the tradition of the Universal Emperor, a Lord of the World. The Hindu kings of India, the birthplace of the idea, had to a large extent been humbled by men of another faith—the Muslim sultans and, now, the Mogul emperors. By definition they could never be the Universal monarch.

The kings of farther India had an additional incentive for

hoping that they might be the great emperor so long prophesied. The Universal Emperor would bring to the world the message of the Buddha and, what was more, might turn out to be the future Buddha, Maitreya the Saviour, whose coming was foretold in the Buddhist scriptures. It was an ambition that transcended mere worldly aspirations. As a rationalisation of the drive for power, it could hardly be bettered. But ambition was not enough. There had to be proof, and not just for the king himself. In Asia as elsewhere, the coming of Saviours was a matter of signs and portents. The problem for a Buddhist king who hoped that he might be the Universal monarch was the question of the attributes by which he could be recognised.

All had been provided for. The Universal Emperor-to-be would have in his possession the Seven Gems. These were the Golden Wheel, the Divine Guardian of the Treasury, the Horse, the Jewel Maiden, the Jewel that wrought Miracles, the General who could never be defeated, and—the White Elephant. What the first six of these symbols actually were is not known. No description—if in fact there ever was one—now exists. But the White Elephants were in the palace of the king of Burma at Pegu, and Ralph Fitch saw at least one of them.

Close to the first gate of the palace were the elephants' stables, if such a plain word can be used for the luxurious quarters assigned to them. The stalls were like houses, elegantly constructed of gilded wood and lined with silks and cushions. Each of the elephants had a retinue of personal servants, men with gold-mounted fly whisks to keep off insects, cooks to prepare food and serve it in 'vessels of silver and gilt'.[29] There were others whose sole duty was to attend the elephant during its daily bath in the river. The progress to the river was itself almost a royal procession.

Preceded by a large white umbrella, that symbol of royalty which it shared only with the king, the elephant was accompanied not only by its personal servants but by a number of courtiers and nobles. Musicians would be playing on drums and flutes and other instruments. When the bathing was over there was another ceremony—'When . . . he [the elephant] cometh out of the river there is a gentleman which doth wash his feet in a silver basin, which is his office given to him by the king.'[30]

On festival occasions there was, of course, much greater display. Fitch does not describe such an occasion, but a later traveller saw what was probably the same elephant when it was in the possession of the king of Arakan, who captured it from the king of Burma thirteen years after Fitch's visit. On festival days, the number of its servants and guards was increased, and a large band accompanied it. The elephant wore a coat of rich crimson velvet, edged with gold and thickly embroidered with large pearls. On its chest a great plate of gold, studded with diamonds and rubies, held the coat together. A heavy gold chain was used as a girth, and the great tusks were banded with gold set with precious stones of many colours.[31]

Fitch comments on the fact that the kings of farther India would fight for the possession of a white elephant, but considers it only as a rare animal towards whose upkeep he and other foreign merchants were forced to contribute. Each had to give the king 'a present of half a ducat, which doth come to a great sum, for that there are many merchants in the city'.[32]

Twice a day, the king himself appeared in a great courtyard inside the palace city to receive petitioners and dispense justice. Actually, the king probably sat at a kind of window while his ministers, courtiers and other officials remained below him in the open court. The petitioners would kneel down some forty paces from the king, holding in their hands 'long leaves of a tree, these leaves are three quarters of a yard long, and two fingers broad, which are written with a sharp Iron made for the purpose'.[33] These were the leaves of the palmyra palm, on which petitions were written with an iron stylus about eight inches long. The scratches were then smeared with a mixture of charcoal and fragrant gum, and afterwards wiped, leaving the lettering filled with the black mixture. The gum acted as a preservative. With the inscribed palm leaf, the petitioner also brought a present, the size and value of which depended on 'the weightiness of their matter'.[34]

When it came to each petitioner's turn, an official took the leaf, read the contents, and approached the king. If the petitioner's plea was acceptable, 'the king accepteth his present and granteth his request; if his suit be not liked of, he returneth with his present for the king will not take it'.[35]

With his usual reticence, Fitch does not say whether he actually had an audience with the king, or not. If, as he says in his published narrative, he left Bengal in November 1586, then the king of Burma would not have been in his capital when Fitch arrived, but away on an expedition against Ayuthia in Siam. But it seems just as likely that Fitch arrived in Burma a year later than he implies. As he kept no diary, the narrative is not necessarily accurate on such points. Certainly, if the king *was* in his capital, Fitch would probably have been received in audience. His presence in Pegu, in whatever disguise he had chosen to wear, could hardly have been kept a secret. He must have had introductions to some of the foreign merchants, perhaps the Portuguese, of whom there were many. It was the king's custom to give audience to foreign visitors, and Fitch would hardly have missed an opportunity to see the ruler of the country at close quarters. Gasparo Balbi, the Venetian jeweller who visited Pegu three years before Fitch, not only had an audience with King Nanda-bayin—who had succeeded his father, Bayin-naung, two years previously—but left a description of the event.

Before the audience, an interpreter was allotted to Balbi, who probably spoke Portuguese. By this time Portuguese had become a kind of diplomatic language for use in dealings with foreigners of all nationalities, and it was the normal practice for a court official who spoke it to be provided to assist those having audience of the king. Balbi and his interpreter approached the outer gate of the audience chamber, where they waited until 'the noise of trumpets was heard, which signified we should see the king and have audience of him'.[36] They then entered a second gate, which opened into a courtyard. There Balbi and his companion knelt upon the ground, 'hands elevated in humble wise, and making a show three times before we rose, of kissing the ground; and three other times before we came near to the place where the king sat with his ministers around him'.[37]

Balbi remained prostrate on the ground some distance from the king, while the king spoke. 'I heard all his speech', recalled Balbi, 'but understood it not.'[38] It was now time for the presentation of gifts. Balbi had brought with him a number of emeralds, which he gave to the interpreter who lifted them above his head, making an obeisance. As soon as the king saw this, the court interpreter—whose title meant 'Lord of His Words'—made a similar obeisance, took the emeralds, and gave them to the king. The king then began a conversation through the interpreter. From what country did Balbi come, he asked? Balbi told him, from Venice, where he had heard of the 'bounty, courtesy, and greatness' of the king.

Nanda-bayin then asked 'in what parts Venice was seated, and what king governed it'? Balbi replied that it had no king but was a republic. Such a thought was unintelligible to an Asian king, and Nanda-bayin 'began to laugh so exceedingly, that he was overcome of the cough, which made him that he could hardly speak'.[39]

Nanda-bayin seems to have taken a liking to Balbi, and asked for news about Philip of Spain, who had just annexed Portugal. He then gave Balbi 'a cup of gold and five pieces of China damask of divers colours'—an unusual piece of kingly generosity, apparently, for it 'was holden a novelty with them that saw it, for it was not the king's custom to present anything to any'.[40] Balbi was also granted exemption from customs duties on the goods he had brought with him.

This pleasant picture of an amused and gracious monarch had its dark counterpart. Though an orthodox Buddhist king, Nanda-bayin was cruel and savage, especially over matters which touched the throne. The possession of the White Elephant was no protection against rebellion; it was, after all, only one of the Seven Gems. Without, at least, the services of the General who could never be defeated, there was always an opening for other people's ambitions. Defiance of the king's authority was commonplace, and the response was a reign of terror. The Talaings were often used as forced labour and were tattooed on the right hand with their name, rank and village. No one was trusted, and the slightest suspicion could result in massacre. Here, the royal family was no exception.

Early in Nanda-bayin's reign, the crown prince struck his wife during an argument with her, and drew blood from her forehead. The princess's father was viceroy of Ava, and to him she sent a bloodstained handkerchief. The viceroy immediately rebelled, and sent letters to the viceroys of

Prome, Toungoo and Chiengmai asking for their help. They refused, sending the letters on to Nanda-bayin. Assuming that there must be a conspiracy among certain of the nobles of his own court, Nanda-bayin ordered their arrest and himself moved off against the rebellious viceroy. Before he left he instructed his officials to prepare to execute not only the suspect nobles but also their families, 'even unto the women great with child, and those in swaddling clothes'.[41] So that the executions should not appear to be merely a matter of vengeance, carried out in precipitate haste, the king instructed his officials to do nothing until they had received from him 'a letter written with his hand in letters of gold'.[42]

The letter was duly received, and the officials took all the nobles and their families—numbering, according to Balbi, around four thousand—to the place of execution, and 'burned them all, so that there was heard nothing but weeping, shriekings, cryings and sobbings'.[43] Balbi was present at the execution and 'saw it with great compassion and grief, that little children without fault should suffer such martyrdom'.[44] Among those sentenced to death was one of the king's chief officials, 'who was last to be burned, yet was freed by the king's order; but his leg was begun to be burnt, so that he was lame'.[45]

Satisfied that he had destroyed any real or potential conspiracy in the capital, Nanda-bayin carried on his march towards Ava, riding on an elephant 'all covered with gold and jewels'.[46] Near Ava, the king and the viceroy met and fought together from the backs of their elephants. The king's elephant was killed under him. The viceroy managed to escape. With his flight, the rebellion collapsed.

When the king was in his capital, he sometimes left the palace on a state elephant, which had 'a fine castle upon him fairly gilded in gold'.[47] On other occasions he travelled in an extravagant palanquin, very much like a small house with pinnacles on top, 'gilded with gold and set with many rubies and sapphires', carried on 'sixteen or eighteen men's shoulders'.[48] The mining of rubies and sapphires was a state monopoly, and the ever-increasing stocks of these precious stones were used to decorate everything royal, from the walls of the palace to the harnesses of the elephants. Some were even stored inside the statues of former kings.

Inside a great walled courtyard in the palace area were 'four houses gilded very richly and covered with lead'.[49] In the first of these was a statue of the king Tabin Shwe-ti, made of gold, 'with a crown of gold on his head full of great rubies and sapphires'.[50] In another there was a statue of silver 'as high as a house; his foot is as long as a man, and he is made sitting, with a crown on his head very rich with stones'.[51] The other two buildings also held very large statues, made of brass, and with crowns on the heads.

In another courtyard were a number of pagodas, each with its gilded images of the Buddha. One of these was the Mahazedi pagoda, constructed by Bayin-naung. Mortared into a wall of its inner shrine was a relic of tremendous sanctity. Possession of this relic, in addition to the White Elephant, made the king of Burma a Buddhist ruler of almost overwhelming prestige. Yet there were some who considered the relic a shameless fraud. Fitch does not mention it, nor does Balbi. Perhaps, as it could not be seen, neither considered it to be of any importance. If so, they were wrong. But though the authenticity of the relic itself might be an open question, the story of its acquisition by Nanda-bayin's father undoubtedly involved a strong element of imposture.

As an orthodox Buddhist monarch, Bayin-naung paid

9. (*right*) Building the Red Fort, Agra. Mogul painting, c. 1600. *Victoria and Albert Museum*, London.

10. (*far right*) Jesuits and Muslim theologians debating before the Emperor Akbar. From an *Akbar-nama* manuscript. *Library of A. Chester Beatty*, Dublin.

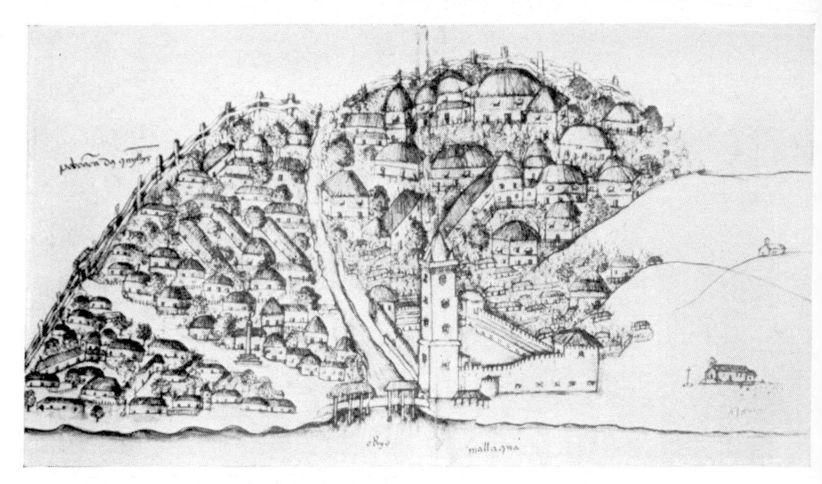

11. Malacca in the mid-sixteenth century. From a manuscript of Gaspar Correia, 'Lendas da India'. *Arquivo Nacional da Torre do Tombo*, Lisbon.

12. Macao c. 1636. From the manuscript of Peter Mundy 'Travels'. *Bodleian Library*, Oxford.

homage to the great shrines of the faith. Among these was the temple of Kandy, in Ceylon. There was preserved one of the most sacred relics of the Buddha himself. At his death, hairs from his head and some of the bones of his body, as well as his teeth, had been taken away by disciples to be enshrined at various centres of the faith. When Ceylon became Buddhist—over a thousand years before the accession of Bayin-naung in Burma—the only surviving tooth was taken to Kandy and placed in a pagoda specially built to receive it.

The Portuguese of the sixteenth century understood this kind of reverence well enough. They had at Goa such relics as the embalmed body of Francis Xavier, even a piece of the True Cross on which Jesus was crucified, and a drop of his blood. When a heathen idol—as they believed—came into their possession, they knew exactly what should be done with it, even if they did have some misgivings on a purely secular plane.

One particular dilemma came about as a result of the profound upsurge of religious feeling at Goa which followed the death of Francis Xavier in 1552. The Portuguese, who had forgotten that part of their mission in Asia was to rescue its people from certain damnation, suddenly became obsessed with righteousness. When, in 1560, the viceroy of the Indies heard that some of Francis's Christian converts were being persecuted by the ruler of Jafna, a small kingdom on the north coast of the island of Ceylon, he decided to send an expedition to save them. He even headed the expedition himself. The attack on Jafna was hard fought, but successful. While the city was being looted, a party came to a temple where they found a tooth set in gold and contained in a casket covered with precious stones. The priests of the temple fought so hard to protect the tooth that the Portuguese became convinced that they had come across something of very great value. When they made enquiries, they were told that it was the Buddha tooth, normally kept in the temple at Kandy, which had been lent to Jafna for a festival.

News that the Portuguese had stolen the tooth soon reached Bayin-naung. Since ascending the throne, he had sent many gifts to the temple of the tooth at Kandy, including a broom made from the hair of himself and his chief queen with which the floor of the sanctuary was to be swept. After the initial shock at learning that the sacred relic was in the hands of the Portuguese, it occurred to the Burmese court that here was an opportunity for the king to gain possession of it for himself. He was still only at the stage of hoping to obtain a white elephant. To be both Master of the Tooth and Lord of the White Elephant would, certainly, make him the greatest king in the world—or, at least, in the Buddhist world. The tooth was of no use to the Portuguese and since, for them, most things had a price, it seemed unlikely that they would refuse a substantial cash offer.

As it happened, a Portuguese ship was in the river about to leave for Goa. Bayin-naung, on the advice of his ministers, sent a letter with the captain addressed to the viceroy at Goa making an offer equivalent to more than £1 million in today's values. The offer was so large that, when he heard of it, the viceroy immediately accepted. It would make a handsome addition to the profits of office. But the viceroy had reckoned without the archbishop, a fanatic who now accused him of being willing to trade in idols. The ecclesiastical authorities, he threatened, would be unlikely to approve. The viceroy marshalled a variety of arguments. The expedition to Jafna had been in the nature of a crusade; the tooth was loot and should be sold to recover expenses. The viceroy's staff supported him. They hoped to be allowed to escort the tooth to Burma and expected substantial presents from the king in return. But the archbishop was immovable. The matter could be settled only by a meeting of the council and of the ecclesiastical court.

The two met and were treated to a sermon by the archbishop on the subject of the Golden Calf and the sin of idolatry. By the end, he had convinced most of those present. But the viceroy was not prepared to give up without a fight. Then, without warning, the archbishop called the viceroy a freemason. As the Inquisition had only recently been established at Goa and was enthusiastically seeking freemasons to burn, even a viceroy could not afford to ignore this threat. The council voted not only that Bayin-naung's offer should be rejected but that the tooth itself should be destroyed.

In 1561, at a public ceremony, the tooth was first ground to powder in a mortar, then burned in a brazier; finally, the ashes were carefully collected, taken out to sea, and distributed. Sacred relics, of course, are not so easily disposed of. By the time news of the Portuguese action reached Burma, it was already known that the tooth was safe. According to one story it had been concealed during the attack on Jafna and a monkey's tooth put in its place. Another story held that, at the moment when it was about to be ground in the archbishop's mortar, a heavenly being substituted a porcelain replica and carried the original back to Ceylon. Yet another described how the tooth had slipped miraculously through the bottom of the mortar, mounted up into the sky, and flown the 750 miles back to Kandy—where it alighted on a lotus flower. One thing at least was sure. Bayin-naung had, for the time being, lost his opportunity of becoming Master of the Tooth.

Many years later, when Bayin-naung had come into

possession of the white elephants, the court astrologers revealed that he was destined to marry a princess of Ceylon and that, with the marriage, would come about some extraordinary good fortune, the precise nature of which they were unable to define. They were, however, sure that the princess would be a daughter of the king of Colombo, a small state near Jafna. Taking his astrologers' advice, Bayin-naung sent envoys to Colombo asking for the king's daughter in marriage. Unfortunately, the king of Colombo had no children. Yet something, it was felt, had to be done to oblige such a great king as the Lord of the White Elephant. The envoys were put off with vague assurances of friendship, and a council of the king's ministers was called to discuss the matter.

The advice of the chief minister was simple. The childless king was accustomed to treat the daughter of one of his counsellors as if she were his own. Why not send her to Burma? The only danger was if the deception was discovered. The counterfeit princess would undoubtedly be executed. But the chief minister knew about the forecast made by the Burmese ruler's astrologers and he suggested that, if the girl were accompanied by a dowry of special appeal to Bayin-naung, he would be unlikely to enquire too deeply into the girl's parentage. Remembering the affair of the tooth, the minister suggested that the dowry should be—the tooth. It was well known that Bayin-naung, despite his successes in battle, despite even his possession of the white elephants, had never ceased to grieve over the matter of the tooth.

At this stage, the king of Colombo is said to have pointed out the obvious fact that he had no tooth to give. The minister's reply was short and to the point. The king had no daughter either. If one could be provided, why not the other?

A few days later, the Burmese envoys were taken with

great secrecy, at night, to visit a golden shrine lit by silver lamps and heavy with incense. The chief minister prostrated himself with unusual devotion before the altar, on which stood a golden casket. When presented for the envoys' inspection, it turned out to be a series of seven caskets. When the innermost was opened it was seen to contain a tooth. This, the envoys were told, was the Kandy tooth. What explanation was given to the envoys for its presence in Colombo is not known. There are conflicting versions. But whatever it was, it was good enough to impress the Burmese. The bait was irresistible. The envoys begged the chief minister to sell the relic to their king. The tooth, they were told, was not for sale. Eventually, after being continually pressed, the minister revealed that it had been the king's intention to give the tooth as his daughter's dowry, but that the matter was being kept secret so that the princess could tell the king of Burma herself. The envoys were asked to keep the secret and agreed, but—as had been anticipated—sent off a messenger by fast ship to Bayin-naung with the tremendous news.

The tooth did not accompany the fake princess when she left for Burma. An auspicious date had to be set by the astrologers and preparations made for the reception. Naturally, the arrival of the princess—the advance guard of a much greater treasure—was particularly brilliant, but the tooth was welcomed in much more impressive style. Bayin-naung himself was rowed down river from Pegu. The casket containing the tooth was placed on a raft under a gilded spire and drawn behind the royal barge by scarlet ropes. Surrounded by boats with musicians aboard, the relic was worshipped by great crowds collected on the banks. At Pegu, the road to the city had been covered with silk. After many days of ceremonies, the tooth, now contained in an even more costly casket, was walled up in the sanctuary of the Mahazedi pagoda. Bayin-naung, quoting the names of some of the greatest of his predecessors, declared: 'Heaven is good to me. Anawrahahta could obtain only a replica tooth from Ceylon, Alaungsithu went to China in vain, but I because of my piety and wisdom, I have been granted this.'[52] A letter from the king of Kandy, pointing out that the sacred relic had never left the temple there and that Bayin-naung had been worshipping a monkey's tooth, was brushed aside. For reasons of state, the tooth could be nothing else but genuine, and the Lord of the White Elephant considered it beneath his dignity to enter into controversy.

As the king was also the Head of the Buddhist Church, the construction and decoration of pagodas was an important and continuing activity. From a Buddhist point of view, the erection of temples was an act of virtue which had its effect on the donor's own destiny. But in a country where the priests were influential, it was also wise policy to keep their favour. The kings of Burma, as model Buddhist monarchs, distributed copies of the scriptures, fed monks, and built monasteries.

The decoration of pagodas used up a vast quantity of gold in the form of plates and gold leaf. Shaped usually like a handbell, the top—as Fitch noted—was always gilded, and 'many of them from top to bottom. Every ten or twelve years they must be new gilded . . . If they did not consume their gold in these vanities, it would be very plentiful and good cheap in Pegu.'[53] It was the custom for the king to break up his coronation regalia and use the jewels to adorn the spire of a pagoda. Tabin Shwe-ti offered his chief queen to the great Shwedagon pagoda and then redeemed her for thirty-six pounds of gold.

The Shwedagon, which stood on the river Irrawaddy

about two days' journey from Pegu, was almost a city in itself. The pagoda, its great bell shape covered with gold, stood over three hundred feet high, and underneath were enshrined eight hairs from the head of the Buddha. Hundreds of smaller shrines surrounded the main structure, which was approached by a number of covered entranceways. At the main entrance stood two great statues of *chinthes*, fabulous animals which Balbi took to be tigers. 'They stand', he wrote, 'with open mouths showing their teeth and tongue, with their claws uplifted and stretched forth, prepared to assail him that looks on them. Concerning these they told me a foolish belief which they have, that they stand there to guard, for if any be so bold to displease the [idol] those tigers would defend him, for he would give them life.'[54]

Fitch found the Shwedagon 'the fairest place, I suppose, that is in the world',[55] its great entrances 'all along set with trees of fruits, in such wise that a man may go in the shade above two miles in length'.[56] For the preaching of sermons there was a great hall with 'three walks in it and forty great pillars gilded which stand between the walks'.[57] Everything seemed to be covered with gold leaf. On most days the main platform and many shrines were crowded with worshippers presenting gifts of flowers and incense, while on feast days 'a man can hardly pass by water or by land for the great press of people, for they come from all places of the kingdom'.[58] In a side hall there was a great bell of bronze which weighed about 289 tons. It was inscribed from top to bottom with letters 'so near together that one toucheth the other . . . but there was no Nation that could understand them, no not the men of Pegu, and they remember not whence, nor how it came thither'.[59] Twenty years after Fitch's visit, a Portuguese adventurer stole the bell to melt down for cannon, but it sank in the river as it was being carried away.

Naturally, in such an important foundation as the Shwedagon, there were thousands of monks. Fitch called them 'Tallipoes', a version of 'Talapoins' used by the Portuguese to describe Buddhist monks in Ceylon and elsewhere. The origin of the word is obscure—the correct word used in Burma was *phungyi*—but most writers followed the Portuguese until well into the nineteenth century without worrying about its accuracy. Fitch thought the monks were 'very strangely apparelled with . . . one thin cloth next to their body of a brown colour, another of yellow, and those two be girded to them with a broad girdle'. The monks went 'bareheaded and barefooted (for none of them weareth shoes) with their right arms bare and a great broad sombrero or shadow in their hands to defend them in Summer from the Sun and in the Winter from the rain'.[60] The dress described by Fitch has scarcely changed to this day.

The monks controlled the schools, and it was there that they found recruits for the Order. If a young man wished to become a monk he was first interrogated many times. Was he prepared to give up his friends 'and the company of all women'? If the answer was yes, 'then he rideth upon a horse about the streets, very richly apparelled, with drums and pipes to show that he leaveth the riches of the world to become a Tallipoe. In a few days after he is carried upon a thing like an horse-litter . . . upon ten or twelve men's shoulders, in the apparel of a Tallipoe, with pipes and drums, and many Tallipoes with him and all his friends, and so they go with him to his house, which standeth without the town, and there they leave him.[61]

These 'houses' were little huts set upon posts and reached by a ladder. The monk, who now had neither possessions nor money, had to beg for his food. 'They go with a great pot, made of wood or fine earth and covered, tied with a broad girdle upon their shoulder . . . They demand nothing, but come to the door, and the people presently do give them some of one thing and some another.'[62] Their food, reports Fitch, consisted of rice, fish and herbs; ordinary people were more catholic in their tastes, eating 'roots, herbs, leaves, dogs, cats, rats, serpents and snakes; they refuse nothing'.[63]

Though Fitch does not mention it, the monks—for all their vows of poverty—were better off than the mass of the people. The endless wars of the kings of Burma impoverished the whole country. Wherever the king went, there were always levies of one kind or another. Ordinary people were made to contribute forced labour. Whole areas of the country had been forcibly depopulated in order to increase the number of inhabitants at the capital, who were used for building works and producing food for the court. The army was in constant need of conscripts, and thousands of young men took the yellow robe of the Buddhist monk in order to avoid being compelled to serve. King Nanda-bayin was so incensed by this that he forced the chief abbot to set up a commission of enquiry, after which many monks were expelled from the Order. Not only the ordinary people suffered from the depredations of the king. In constant need of money, he exacted tribute from the petty rulers of tributary states. He also took their daughters for his harem and their young men for service in his palaces. Artisans and craftsmen were in particular demand, fine lacquer workers from Chiengmai, jewellers from Mokeik.

A traveller such as Ralph Fitch, coming from the cold of northern Europe, with its dirty and insanitary towns, was dazzled not only by the gold and jewels and the warm sun, but by the cleanliness of the towns and people in comparison with those of Europe. The city of Pegu, with its wide shady streets, was almost a paradise when contrasted with Elizabethan London. The criticisms of such men are few, and mainly concerned with strange customs and heathen practices. The myth of the Gorgeous East was safe with them. In any case, it was with the rich and powerful that Fitch's employers expected to do business. Fitch saw only the potential market—and it was certainly an impressive one.

Not content with merely observing the king and capital, the monks, and the great shrines of the heartland of the kingdom, Fitch made a journey to one of the outlying provinces, Chiengmai, one of the Shan states which had been occupied by Bayin-naung after a series of campaigns in 1556/59. The journey was somewhat hazardous, for the area was in almost continual rebellion. Fitch probably travelled to Chiengmai—which was about two hundred miles from Pegu—by way of the coast, south-east from Pegu, crossing the valley of the Salween river. It would be a roundabout way, but possibly safer than the more direct route overland.

Chiengmai, which was to be lost by Nanda-bayin a few years later, was then governed by his brother, Tharrawadymin. It took Fitch twenty-five days to reach the city, and he found it a 'very great and fair town',[64] the women much lighter in colour than those of Pegu. To the markets of Chiengmai came 'merchants out of China and bring great store of musk, gold, silver and many other things of China work'.[65] The people ate no wheat, but there was plenty of rice. Apparently they did not drink the milk of the water buffalo, 'as they do in all other places'.[66]

At Chiengmai, Fitch learned that when people fell ill they made a vow of an offering of food 'unto the devil if they escape',[67] and when they recovered held a great banquet to which their friends brought gifts of fruit and fragrant 'arrecaes'.[68] This last was betel, or *pan*, the sliced nut of the areca palm rolled with a little lime and spices in a leaf of the betel vine, chewed by most of the population of south and south-east Asia. It stained the teeth, but Fitch also noted that it was considered fashionable to blacken the teeth even more. This seemed to him very odd, and on a par with the Burmese habit of tattooing themselves and pulling the hair out of their faces with little pincers made especially for the purpose.

If a sick man was unfortunate enough to die, having had his offering to the 'devil' rejected, his body was 'carried upon a great frame made like a tower, with a covering all gilded with gold, made of canes, carried by fourteen or sixteen men, with drums and pipes and other instruments playing before him, to a place out of the town and there is burned'.[69] The unburnt bones were later collected and buried. The only sign of mourning apart from a certain amount of wailing and crying was a substantial feast and the shaving of the heads of the relatives, a sacrifice usually made only on the occasion of a death, 'for they much esteem of their hair'.[70]

Another custom of the countries of Indo-China retailed by Fitch has all the amusing obscenity of the traditional traveller's tale. The men, he reported, 'wear bunches of little round balls in their privy members . . . They cut the skin and so put them in, which they do when they be twenty or twenty-five.'[71] Some, he said, were made of 'brass and some of silver, but those of silver be for the king and his noblemen; these are gilded and made with great cunning and ring like a little bell'.[72] Lesser men had to make do with lead, which though cheaper 'ring but little'.[73] The king 'sometimes taketh his out and giveth them to his noblemen as a great gift, and because he hath used them they esteem them greatly'.[74] What the purpose of all this is supposed to have been is by no means clear, though Fitch was sure it had some connection with virility—'for they say the women do desire them'. He also says that they were 'invented because they should not abuse the male sex, for in times past all those countries were [so] given to that villainy that they were very scarce of people'[75]—an oblique way, perhaps, of warning young Elizabethans against the dire consequences of masturbation.*

From Chiengmai Fitch returned to Pegu, and as his final anecdote from the land of the Lord of the White Elephant tells of the Burmese way of settling a difficult case at law. The judges, 'if they have a suit which is so doubtful that they cannot well determine it, put two long canes into the water where it is very deep, and both the parties go into the water by the poles, and there sit men to judge. The two parties then dive into the water and he which remaineth longest under the water doth win the suit.'[76]

*Another and far more detailed explanation of the technique and purpose of this bizarre practice is given by the Florentine merchant, Francesco Carletti, who was in Indo-China a few years after Fitch during a voyage round the world. His reports to the Grand Duke of Tuscany were written down in a series of *Ragionamenti* (Chronicles). An English translation of the manuscript in the Biblioteca Angelica has been published under the title of *My Voyage round the World*, translated by Herbert Weinstock, London 1965. Carletti's version of the Fitch story is on pp. 181–83.

VIII

Gateway to Cathay

While in the kingdom of Pegu, Fitch obviously decided that, as he was so near the Portuguese settlement of Malacca, he must make his way there. Malacca was the gateway to China, that mysterious land of Cathay, and it is possible that Fitch still carried the letter to the emperor of China which Elizabeth had given Newbery on their departure for the East. Perhaps Fitch planned a visit there. If so, Malacca was the place to start from, for ships came there from Macao, the Portuguese trading post in south China. As usual, Fitch does not disclose his thoughts or intentions. 'The 10th of January I went from Pegu to Malacca' is all he is prepared to say,[1] and the journey itself is dismissed in a few words.

On his journey Fitch passed the port of Martaban and then sailed down the coast of Tenasserim. The island of Tavoy, he notes, exported a 'great store of tin which serveth all India',[2] but he does not mention the famous arrack, the palm wine of Mergui. This wine was known to Europeans as *nipa* or *nyper*, from the Malay word for the palm itself, and the English word 'nip'—as in the phrase 'take a nip of brandy'—may possibly have had its origin here. The effects of arrack were by no means confined to the convivial, though much seems to have been drunk solely for pleasure. Cesar Federici tells of the large quantities exported of this 'excellent wine, which is made of the flower of a tree called

Nyper'. As 'clear as crystal', nyper wine was good for the stomach, but it also had 'an excellent gentle virtue, that if one were rotten with the French pox, drinking good store of this he shall be whole again'.[3]

Federici was not just repeating hearsay, for he had seen the properties of nyper proved to his own satisfaction. When he was at Cochin in south India a friend of his, 'whose nose began to drop away with that disease', was 'counselled of the doctors of physic that he should go to Tenasserim and that he should drink of the nyper wine, as much as he could before it was distilled'.[4] Apparently, before the process of distilling the wine was 'most delicate' and presumably at its most medically effective. Federici's friend took the doctors' advice and was later seen 'with a good colour and sound'.[5] With these useful qualities, it was not surprising that nyper wine should be 'esteemed much in the Indies'[6] and very expensive.

Fitch arrived in Malacca on 8 February, the first Englishman to set foot in Malaya and to see the great trading port through which the Portuguese brought the spices of the Indonesian archipelago and the luxuries of China. The Portuguese had first come to Malacca when it was the capital of a great Muslim kingdom, dominating the trade routes and rich with the profits. As they probed outwards from India towards the Spice Islands and China, the Portuguese sailed into the harbour of Malacca in September 1509. They were not welcomed. The inhabitants thought they were 'white Bengalis'. The sultan's first minister considered their leader, one Diego Lopez de Siqueira, 'a person of no manners', as he insisted on throwing a gold chain around the minister's neck. More importantly, the local traders and merchants believed they might be a threat to their monopolies.

The minister seems to have listened to the merchants, for

it was decided that the Portuguese and their fleet should be seized. Some twenty Portuguese were taken, but Siqueira managed to escape, burning two of his ships because he had not enough men to sail them. Among those who escaped with him was Ferdinand Magellan, the famous navigator. The imprisonment of the Portuguese sailors was an excuse for later Portuguese aggression, but they would most probably have taken Malacca anyway. The Portuguese were out for trade and had no hesitation about fighting for it. Malacca was full of merchants from all over the Far East. In its harbour rode ships from as far away as China. These great junks, wrote Magellan's brother-in-law, Duarte Barbosa, 'differ much from the fashion of ours, being built of very thick timber, so that when they are old a new planking can be laid over the former . . . so they remain strong. The cables and all the shrouds . . . are made of canes which grow in the country.'[7] Some of these vessels were very large indeed, a number of them carrying as many as two thousand men—immense compared with the tiny Portuguese ships of the time. Altogether, Malacca was 'the richest seaport with the greatest number of wholesale merchants and abundance of shipping and trade that can be found in the whole world'.[8] It was the control of this trade that the Portuguese were determined to have for themselves.

In May 1511, the Portuguese conqueror of the East, Alfonso d'Albuquerque, sailed from Cochin in western India with a fleet of eighteen ships and eight hundred Portuguese fighting men. The situation in Malacca had not remained static during the Portuguese preparations. The sultan had deposed his powerful minister and had him executed, not—as he was to pretend to Albuquerque—for attacking and imprisoning the Portuguese, but because he and his family had threatened the throne. Just the same, the sultan would not give up the Portuguese prisoners as he believed them to be valuable hostages against attack. But the sultan understood neither the character of Albuquerque nor of the captives, who smuggled out a letter declaring their willingness to die for their king and their God.

Albuquerque demanded the release of the prisoners. The sultan temporised. Albuquerque burned all the ships in the harbour except five Chinese junks, and some houses on the shore. The prisoners were instantly released. But the sultan was preparing for war. Stockades were erected on shore. According to a report from a Chinese merchant, there were more than twenty thousand fighting men in the city, twenty war elephants, and artillery. Albuquerque took the initiative, landing men from one of the Chinese junks which had been offered by its captain. The fighting was heavy, but after several days the Portuguese took the city. Their morale had been high, but they had also been helped by the neutrality of many of the foreign merchants in the city, who had grievances against the sultan and his officials. The sultan's army was mainly composed of Javanese mercenaries who had not been paid for some time and consequently did not fight particularly well.

Immediately after the taking of the city, Albuquerque began the erection of a fort. It stood next to the sea so that reinforcements could be easily supplied. As the years went by, the fortifications became more and more elaborate. Great walls of stone and mortar faced the water. Strong towers with gun emplacements were erected at key points and named after the Virgin Mary and other saints. Some of the stone for construction was taken from buildings and tombs in the palace quarter of the city.

Within the fort area the Portuguese constructed a small European town in stone. There were a governor's palace

13. Portuguese ship taking the first traders and missionaries to Japan. From a Japanese lacquer screen of c. 1600. *Victoria and Albert Museum*, London.

14. Pepper harvest in Malabar, a late mediaeval view. From the fourteenth-century illuminated manuscript known as the 'Livre des Merveilles'. *Bibliothèque Nationale*, Paris.

A priueledge for fifteene yeares g
to certayne adventurers for the discoverie
for the East Indies.

Elizabeth by the grace of god Queene of Englande ffraunce and I
of the faith &c. To all our officers ministers and subiectes and to all other people
this our realme of Englande as elsewhere under our obedience and iurisdiction, or ot
these our lres patentes shalbe seene shewed or reade, greetinge. Whereas our moste de
Cosen George Earle of Cumberlande, and our welbeloved subiectes Sir John Harte
Knighte, Sir John Spencer of London knight, Sir Edward Michelborne knight,
Cavendishe esquire, Paule Banninge, Robert Lee, Leonarde Holiday, John Watte,
Edwarde Holmeden Robert Hampson Thomas Smythe, and Thomas Cambell

15. Beginning of the Charter of the first English East India Company. From a photograph in the possession of the India Office Library, *Foreign and Commonwealth Office*, London.

and a town hall, five churches and two hospitals, a Jesuit college and a number of other religious foundations. All this for a Portuguese population of about three hundred men and their families, quartered in pleasant houses with gardens within the ramparts. Outside the fort area was the Malay town, with a central market place where the Javanese, who supplied Malacca with most of its food, had their warehouses and stalls. The Javanese, in spite of the fact that they were periodically at war with Malacca both before and after the coming of the Portuguese, would not give up their lucrative monopoly. Every year, according to one Portuguese traveller, there arrived at Malacca more than two hundred large junks from Java, 'loaded with common rice, every kind of grain, garlic, butter, oils, honey, wax, cassia fistula, a little cinnamon, tamarinds, coconuts, fowls, birds, saffron . . . large quantities of meat, and pickled and dried fish'.[9] Foolishly, the Portuguese made no attempt to encourage the local inhabitants to cultivate the lands around Malacca. When supplies from Java were interrupted by war, the Portuguese were threatened with starvation on more than one occasion.

The rest of the inhabitants were of many races, Tamils from south India, Gujaratis from the west coast, and Chinese. But Fitch comments only upon the Malays. They were 'a kind of proud people', he wrote. 'They go naked with a cloth around their middle and a little roll of cloth about their heads.'[10] Each of the races occupied its own quarter and was administered by a native official appointed by the Portuguese 'Captain of the Fortress', who was also known by the grandiloquent title of 'Governor of the South'.

The Portuguese soon established themselves as the principal traders. No vessel was allowed to use the straits without a licence from the Portuguese at Malacca. The Portuguese imposed their will by action against anyone who tried to violate their self-assumed rights. Ships trying to avoid Malacca were hunted down, their cargoes confiscated, their crews enslaved, and the ships themselves burned. While there was no opposition from other Europeans, Malacca remained the great entrepôt of east Asian trade. From the Malay peninsula and the east-coast ports of Sumatra came pepper, tin, gold, eagle wood, bezoar stones, resin, ivory, rhinoceros horns, birds' nests, rice, and rattan canes. The ships that brought these commodities carried back with them from the warehouses of Malacca the cloth of India, from Coromandel, Bengal and Surat, fine porcelain from China, and gold coins. From Borneo and Java, from Macassar and the islands of the Indonesian archipelago, the ships were laden with Javanese batiks, slaves, sandalwood, tortoise-shell and rice. The Portuguese brought from Siam and Cambodia benzoin, gum-lac, gold and rice, in exchange for cloth. From the Spanish islands of the Philippines, they brought white and brown sugar, tortoise-shell and gold, in exchange for slaves and cloth. For the Chinese market there was pepper and ivory, rhinoceros horn—that famed aphrodisiac—sandalwood, incense, bright red coral, glowing amber, slaves and camphor. The ships brought back all manner of China wares, tin, iron and porcelain.

To the exchange trade of the Far East the Portuguese brought from Goa and Cochin not only those high-demand Indian cloths, but incense from Arabia, ivory from Africa, and wine from Portugal for the rulers of the East. In return they took luxury goods of all kinds, and many spices for the markets of Europe as well as for India and the Near East. In fact, though the Portuguese had gone to Asia in search of spices and other goods to resell in Europe, by the time Ralph Fitch was investigating the markets for the magnates of

Elizabethan England the Portuguese were making much more profit out of inter-Asian trade than they had ever anticipated making in Europe.

They did not do so without opposition from Asians. If Fitch arrived in Malacca in the year 1587, as seems likely, he did so during one of the periodic conflicts with the Malay state of Johore. Portuguese relations with Johore were, to say the least, variable. Sometimes Malacca and Johore were allies against the main indigenous power, that of Acheh. With their occupation of Malacca, the Portuguese inherited and then enhanced the threat posed by the ambitions of the Muslim sultans of Acheh. Their attempts to control the whole of the transit trade of the area and their persecution of Muslim merchants who had once controlled that trade, drove many of the latter to Acheh in Sumatra. With their coming, Acheh had expanded and taken over the principal pepper-growing areas of the island.

As Acheh grew richer it became more powerful and soon began a long series of attacks on Portuguese Malacca. The most serious had been in 1547 when an Achinese fleet had entered the harbour of Malacca and burnt Portuguese vessels, landing a force at night. But the Achinese did not remain. They returned to their ships and the Achinese admiral sent a challenge to the Captain of the Fort, written in the blood of seven captured fishermen, who—suitably mutilated—accompanied the letter. The Portuguese were short of men and provisions, and the commander was unwilling to accept the challenge. In Malacca at the time was Francis Xavier who, in an impassioned speech, managed to persuade the Portuguese to make their ships ready for battle, whatever the shortcomings of the arsenal and the commissariat. Unfortunately, when the five galleys that were available set sail to find the Achinese, who had departed to attack shipping further up the coast, one of them immediately sank. This seemed to settle Xavier's assurances of divine help, and a mutiny took place.

Yet the immense hypnotic power of Xavier's faith, which was continually attested to by those who met him, once again worked effectively. 'Put your trust in God,' he said. 'You have lost one galley but He will send you two.' There were, he assured them, two galleys on the way. Those who were sceptical were confounded by the arrival of two ships commanded by one of the Portuguese mercenaries employed by the king of Pegu. The story of what followed helps to demonstrate that peculiar mixture of the mercenary and the missionary, of alternating genuflexions to God and Mammon, which summarised the nature of Portuguese adventuring in Asia. The commander of the two ships had no intention of entering the harbour at Malacca, but was sailing past. Xavier insisted that he must be stopped and suggested that he himself should go and divert the ships to the aid of Malacca.

When Xavier reached the vessels, the Portuguese commander received him with great deference. 'What can I do to serve Your Reverence?' he asked. 'I adjure you by the Five Wounds to join forces with us against the infidels of Acheh,' replied Xavier. The commander said that it had been his intention not to put in to Malacca at all, in order to avoid customs duties, but since such a saintly person as Xavier requested his assistance in the service of God he was willing to give it—though only if Xavier would procure for him a certificate signed by the governor and the customs officers that he was exempted from all dues. This businesslike attitude did not upset Xavier at all. The certificate was produced, and with the two new vessels the Portuguese force set out to find the Achinese.

When the two fleets met, superior Portuguese seamanship and fire power once again won the contest, but the news of the victory was a long time in reaching the anxious Portuguese at Malacca. Then, one Sunday, Xavier ended his sermon and turned towards the great crucifix over the altar. 'Love of my soul,' he cried, 'we supplicate you not to abandon us.' After a few moments' pause, his head lowered, Xavier suddenly raised a face lit up with joy and spoke loudly to the congregation. 'Gentlemen, say a Pater Noster and an Ave Maria in thanks for the great victory Our Lord has granted us against the enemies of the faith.' Six days later a messenger arrived with the news that, at the moment when the vision of victory had come to Xavier at Malacca, the Portuguese had defeated the Achinese fleet.[11]

But it was not the end of the conflict with Acheh. Malacca was threatened many times, though the attacks were always beaten off, sometimes with great difficulty. Five years before Fitch's visit, Acheh had attacked Johore and, in their own interests, the Portuguese had sent a force to assist the sultan in repelling the Achinese. In return, the sultan visited Malacca to thank the governor, and 'a trade in spices and metals, including a large quantity of tin'[12] grew up between Johore and Malacca. But two years later the Portuguese began to interfere with the shipping of Johore, and the sultan sank junks in the Singapore straits to prevent Portuguese shipping from using them, and blockaded the land approaches to Malacca. In 1586 an attack from Johore was driven off after bloody fighting. Negotiations between the two sides failed to bring agreement, and in July 1587, after receiving reinforcements from Goa, the Portuguese began an attack on the great port of Johore Lama, taking the city in the following month. This victory was thought to be so important that news of it was sent to the great German banking house of

Fugger. But there is no mention of it in Fitch's narrative which becomes, at this stage, even more sketchy than before.

Of course, Fitch was more interested in trade and the prospects of trade. But in the Indies trade and war were inseparable, as the English were to find out. Fitch does not say, either, with whom he stayed when in Malacca, though it was presumably with Portuguese merchants. Perhaps he had obtained letters from his Portuguese acquaintances at Hugli and Pegu. His presence must have been known to the Portuguese authorities at Malacca, who did not act against him despite instructions from King Philip that no Englishman was to be allowed to land at Malacca. By this time, Fitch probably spoke Portuguese well and he may have passed himself off as a continental European. Certainly, he was taking notes and observing the extent of Portuguese trade. It was significent in the light of future events that, as this first Englishman looked outwards upon the seas of the East Indies, noting the great trade carried on from Malacca, another Englishman, Thomas Cavendish, crossing the Pacific, had reached the Spice Islands and passed through the straits of Macassar and Bali. Together, the experiences of land traveller and sailor were to contribute to the decision of English merchants to penetrate those areas once thought to be the exclusive property of the Portuguese.

Fitch was particularly, and rightly, interested in Portuguese trade with China and Japan. The centre of that trade was the town of Macao, which had been established by arrangement with local Chinese officials on a tiny peninsula in the estuary of the Canton river in 1557. The first Portuguese settlers there called the place *povoacao do Nome de Deos na China*, the 'settlement of the Name of God in China', but this and its variants were too long for ordinary use and the town was usually known by the Portuguese version of the

Chinese name Amangao, derived from Ama, the Chinese goddess. The Portuguese had found early in their excursions into the China seas that they could make as much profit from selling spices to the Chinese as they could to Europe.

Their first ventures into the China trade had suffered from the activities of Portuguese pirates who had sailed up the Canton river in 1519, landed troops, and begun to erect a fort, before they were driven off by a Chinese fleet. But, as some compensation for the merchants, Japan had been discovered accidentally by three Portuguese deserters in 1542. For a time, this diverted Portuguese attention from trade with mainland China. The difficulty of sailing unwieldy craft from Malacca to Japan during the typhoon season, however, finally convinced the Portuguese that they needed a trading base in China, where they could buy adequate supplies of the Chinese raw and woven silks which were in great demand in Japan. Diplomacy, suitably oiled with bribes, resulted in the establishment of Macao.

Though early trade had been carried on as a free-for-all, the usual Portuguese practice of making trade a royal monopoly and granting privileges as a reward for services was in force by 1550. In charge of the monopoly was the Captain-Major of the Voyage of China and Japan—an officer appointed annually by the king. The privilege was usually bestowed on individuals, but on occasion it could be conferred on one of the Portuguese municipalities in Asia or some deserving religious institution. The office-holder could, and often did, sell the privilege to the highest bidder. The profits were vast, especially as direct relations between China and Japan were virtually non-existent, and a ban had been placed on trade by the Chinese emperor in 1480. This left trade open to smugglers and, later, to an alliance between Chinese officials and the Portuguese.

The demand for Chinese silks in Japan was considerable, and the Portuguese were able to buy cheap and sell dear. As Japan seemed to have nothing worth exporting, cargoes were sold for gold and silver bullion which not only paid for the original consignments but also for the Indian and other products in demand in China. There was also a considerable profit to be made on the fluctuating values of gold and silver in the Indies. All this Fitch learned in Malacca. 'When the Portugals', he wrote, 'go from Macao in China to Japan, they carry much white silk, gold, musk and porcelains; and they bring from thence nothing but silver. They have a great carrack which goeth thither every year, and she bringeth from thence every year above six hundred thousand cruzadoes'[13]—a very large sum in terms of the times, and several millions of pounds at today's values.

Fitch's 'great carrack' was one of the largest ships afloat at the time, a giant of over a thousand tons similar to the *Madre de Deus* captured by the English in the Azores in 1592 on its homeward journey from India, which was estimated at sixteen hundred tons. The best and most seaworthy of these ships were built at the Indo-Portuguese yards at Goa, Daman, Bassein and Cochin. The material used was teak, a wood of great durability which was also resistant to worm-rot. Possibly Fitch saw one of these great vessels at Malacca, for it was usual for the Japan carrack to call in there on its way from Goa.

The normal routine of the annual Japan voyage started at Goa in April or May. On board would be the captain-major, and a cargo of woollens, scarlet cloth, fine crystal and glass-ware, Flemish clocks, Portuguese wines, Indian chintzes, cotton lengths, calico and printed cloth. On arrival at Malacca, part of this cargo would be exchanged for spices, the scented wood of sandal, eagle, and aloes, the hides of deer and sharkskins from Siam, and the many strange drugs of the Asian pharmacopoeia. The length of the ship's stay at Malacca depended upon whether or not the carrack had missed the monsoon. When it finally got away, the journey was usually made without a stop to Macao.

At Macao the cargo was already being prepared. The mart was at Canton, up river from Macao, and the Chinese authorities would permit business to be conducted only twice a year, in January and June, at special fairs arranged for the occasion. The Portuguese merchants were severely restricted while at Canton. Fitch notes that, when they arrived there, 'they come in at the gate of the city', and 'they must enter their names in a book, and when they go out at night they must put their names'.[14] They must not, he goes on, 'lie in the town all night, but must lie in their boats without the town'.[15] At the end of the trading period, the Portuguese had to leave or be arrested. 'The Chinians', Fitch comments, 'are very suspicious and do not trust strangers,' adding his own observation on the unofficial relationship between the Portuguese and the local Chinese: 'It is thought that the king [of China] does not know that any strangers come into his country.'[16]

Unfortunately, the Canton trading seasons did not coincide with the winds that brought the carrack from Malacca. The great ship would arrive in port between June and August, and though some stocks would have been held at Macao from the Chinese sales, the carrack's cargo had to be sold in order to pay for the purchases destined for Japan. It was, therefore, usually necessary for the carrack to wait at Macao for ten or twelve months. The vessel was too large to go up river to Canton, and anchored in the Macao roads while the silks and other goods were brought down the Pearl river or the West river in lighters.

In the year following its arrival in the Macao roads, the carrack—laden with silks and other China wares—would leave for Japan with the south-west monsoon between June and August, and arrive off southern Kyushu after a voyage lasting between twelve and thirty days. Usually, the carrack carried a Chinese pilot, one of the men from the province of Fukien, who had a wide knowledge of the seas between the Chinese mainland and Japan. Before 1571, the landfall in Japan was one of a number of ports, but in that year the town of Nagasaki became the official port for the Macao trade and the most frequent port of call.

Arriving at Nagasaki, the carrack unloaded its cargo and remained there until the north-east monsoon broke at the end of October or the beginning of November. The return cargo was, in Fitch's time and after, mainly silver bullion, but some exotic goods were also loaded. Fine lacquer cabinets, boxes and furniture, painted screens of gold leaf, paper, swords and kimonos, all had a small but ready sale in Goa and in Europe. A proportion of the silver was usually unloaded at Macao in order to finance at least part of the next year's cargo of silks. With a fresh cargo of silk and China wares, the carrack would then prepare to leave for Malacca and Goa. The round voyage from Goa to Japan and back would take as long as three years if the monsoon winds were missed.

Fitch may have talked with men who had made the voyage to Japan, but he records nothing of what he may have heard about the country. Of China and the Chinese, he notes that the emperor was seldom seen by his subjects, that in fact 'they may not look up to that place where he sitteth'.[17] When he went into the streets, the emperor was 'carried upon a great chair . . . gilded very fair, wherein there is made a little house with a lattice to look out at, so that he may see them but they may not look up at him'.[18] Apart from the fact that the Chinese 'do write downwards and they do write with a fine pencil made of dog's or cat's hair',[19] the only other information Fitch thought worth mentioning concerned their funeral ceremonies.

'When they mourn,' he wrote, 'they wear white thread shoes and hats of straw. The man doth mourn for his wife two years, the wife for her husband three years, the son for his father a year and his mother two years. All the time which they mourn they keep the dead [body] in the house, the bowels being taken out and filled with lime, and coffined.'[20] When the period of mourning was over, they carried the body out, 'playing and piping', and burned it. 'And when they return they pull off their mourning weeds and marry at their pleasure. A man may keep as many concubines as he will, but one wife only.'[21]

Why Fitch finally decided that he could not make the journey to China is not known, but he would have learned that access to the emperor himself was out of the question. Even if it had been possible, the Portuguese would have done their best to prevent anyone other than themselves reaching his court. In fact, the Portuguese had no contact with the imperial capital. The first Portuguese envoy to reach Peking was also the last, for on his arrival he had been arrested and sent back to Canton, where he died a prisoner in 1523. After that, the Portuguese had contented themselves with dealing with local officials. What is known of Fitch's character—his determination, against considerable odds, to journey to as many places as he could, and his apparent fearlessness—suggests that the physical dangers involved in attempting a visit to China would hardly have deterred him. Perhaps he was running short of money; he gives no indication of how he paid his way. But it is more likely that he decided it was time to return home and put the information he had managed to collect at the service of his employers.

It was perhaps for this reason, above all, that he made no attempt to investigate the points of origin of the spice trade, or to examine at source the possibilities of doing business in competition with the Portuguese. He had seen the extent and the profit of that trade at Goa, Hugli, and at Malacca. There was little else he, an independent merchant, could do, especially if he were short of funds and in danger if the Portuguese should decide to arrest him. The tales he would have heard at Malacca—of the rulers of the islands of the Indonesian archipelago, of the pirates that infested the eastern seas—may well have convinced his businesslike mind that the risks were, relatively, too high. His main purpose had been achieved. He had spied out the land, and it was his duty to ensure that the information he had gained should not be lost.

In his published narrative, Fitch gives few precise details of the trade of the islands, or even of what he had heard about them and their rulers. In the section covering his stay at Malacca, only three items, he decides, are interesting enough to be included. 'Laban', he writes, 'is an island among the Javas; from whence come the diamonds of the new water; and they find them in the rivers, for the king will not suffer them to dig the rock.'[22] By Laban, Fitch may have meant Labuan, an island off the coast of north Borneo. 'Jamba', too, he says, 'is an island among the Javas . . . from whence come diamonds.' Even more interestingly, 'the King hath a mass of earth which is gold; it groweth in the middle of a river. And when the King doth lack gold they cut part of the earth and melt it, whereof cometh gold. This mass of earth', he adds, 'doth appear but once a year, which is when the water is low; and this is in the month of April.'[23] As for 'Bima'—yet another 'island among the Javas', though this one apparently had neither gold nor diamonds—'the women travail and labour as our men do in England, and the men keep house and go where they will'.[24]

Bima is certainly an island, a very small one in the Lesser Sundas, but it is by no means unique in the use of female labour. The nearest name to Jamba is Jambi, which is not an island. Fitch probably remembered imperfectly, for it is unlikely that he took notes, some of the many tales he heard at Malacca. His own veracity is not in question, and the stories themselves are not untrue, though their truth is of the general, rather than the particular, variety.

On 29 March 1588, the first Englishman to penetrate to the margins of farther Asia left Malacca on the first stage of the long journey home.

IX

The journey home

From Malacca, Fitch retraced his steps, going up the coast of Tenasserim and Arakan to the port of Martaban and the Burmese capital of Pegu. He may have considered making the tedious journey across northern India and proceeding by land through the Near East, the route Newbery—of whose fate Fitch knew nothing—had chosen. Fitch remained at Pegu until 17 September 1588 and then was able to take a ship from the port of Bassein to Bengal. He does not say at which port in Bengal he landed, but on the way there he escaped 'many dangers by reason of contrary winds',[1] and arrived at some time in November. There he seems to have decided to take the risk of going by sea in a Portuguese vessel to the Portuguese settlement of Cochin in south India, from where he could embark for the Persian Gulf. It was a brave decision, and typical of Fitch; if he were to be recognised by the Portuguese as one of the Englishmen who had escaped from the authorities at Goa, he would certainly be imprisoned—if nothing worse. Perhaps he relied on the facts that he now spoke Portuguese well, and that his travels had changed his appearance, to help him escape detection. Unfortunately, having made his decision, he found that there were no ships in Bengal to take him to Cochin, and he was compelled to wait until February 1589 before he could embark.

The voyage through the Bay of Bengal to the first landfall in Ceylon was neither pleasant nor free from danger. The passengers, many merchants among them, 'endured great extremity for lack of fresh water',[2] and 'the weather was extreme hot . . . and we had many calms'.[3] Nevertheless, 'it pleased God that we arrived in Ceylon on 6 March, where we stayed five days to water and to furnish ourselves with other necessary provisions'.[4]

The port at which Fitch arrived was Colombo, the headquarters of Portuguese activity on the island. The Portuguese had first set foot in Ceylon only eight years after the visit of Vasco da Gama to the mainland of India in 1498, but it was some time before they established themselves, building a fort at Colombo by permission of the king of Kotte in 1518. Kotte was the most important of the three kingdoms which at that time divided up Ceylon. But the Portuguese had their problems. Other merchants resented their presence and made trouble for them with the king. In 1524 the Portuguese abandoned the fort, returning only after a palace revolution had produced a request from one of the contending parties for Portuguese assistance. In payment they received an annual consignment of some fourteen thousand pounds of cinnamon.

This profitable arrangement continued until 1551 when a new king, with the support of the Portuguese, succeeded to the throne. Six years later, the king was converted to Christianity, which—though it helped to confirm Portuguese supremacy—antagonised the Buddhist population and invited the emergence of someone to champion their interests and that of their faith. Until almost the end of the century, the Portuguese and their puppet found themselves in conflict with rivals for power, and for most of the time the rule of the Portuguese extended no further than the walls of Colombo. Even that was threatened by a number of sieges, the most serious of which was beaten off during the year before Fitch's visit.

It had been mounted by Rajasinha, the ruler of Sitawaka, who with his father and predecessor had expanded his dominion to cover not only most of Kotte but also the kingdom of Kandy. On the conquest of that kingdom in 1581, the ruler had fled to Portuguese protection at Colombo. In 1587, Rajasinha decided that he was strong enough to attack the fort there. He had, Fitch reported, 'an hundred thousand men and many elephants', and though the Sinhalese did not wear body armour, 'yet many of them be good with their pieces, which be muskets'.[5] Fitch also heard of Rajasinha that when he 'talketh with any man he standeth upon one leg and setteth the other foot upon his knee with his sword in his hand; it is not their order for the king to sit but to stand. His apparel is a fine painted cloth made of cotton . . . about his middle; his hair is long and bound with a little fine cloth about his head; all the rest of his body is naked. His guard are one thousand men, which stand around him and he in the middle, and when he marcheth many of them go before him and the rest go behind.'[6]

Fitch no doubt obtained this information from some Portuguese of his acquaintance in Colombo, but he records nothing about the siege itself, which had almost resulted in the surrender of the Portuguese. Rajasinha had carefully prepared his attack. A lake which protected one side of the fort was drained—a clever move, as the Portuguese defences were weak on that flank. A sortie by the defenders relieved the pressure for a while, and the arrival of reinforcements from Goa helped, but the garrison was still in great danger. Rajasinha's forces attacked the walls, but were at last driven back with considerable losses. It had been a close and terrible fight. As an eye-witness noted, when day dawned it was 'for our people as great a joy as comes to those that in some storm thought themselves lost in the darkness of the night, when the day breaks upon them clear and serene'.[7]

This was only a respite, and a more alarming enemy was already within the gates. The draining of the lake had reduced the city's water supply. At the time of the siege there were some sixty thousand people inside the fortifications. An outbreak of plague soon escalated the casualties. There were so many that it was believed that Rajasinha had poisoned the wells. The situation was so serious that the Portuguese decided on a diversion. An attack was made on Kandy by an expedition which was accompanied by the heirs of the late king. It was successful. The old dynasty was restored in Kandy, and the pressure on Colombo was relieved. When further reinforcements arrived from Goa, Rajasinha finally withdrew from the siege, burning his stockades. When the Portuguese defenders came to examine the engineering works which had been constructed to drain the lake, they were astounded by their sophistication.

Fitch stayed at Colombo for only five days. As well as cinnamon, 'which smelleth very sweet'[8] and was the main reason for Portuguese interest in the island, Ceylon was famous for 'rubies, sapphires and spinels . . . but the King will not suffer the inhabitants to dig for them lest his enemies should know of them and make wars against him, and so drive him out of the country for them'[9]—an interesting conceit, which hardly squared up with the fact that the king in question had almost destroyed the Portuguese presence in Ceylon as well as most of his actual or potential enemies.

During his short stay, Fitch observed of the people that 'all of them be black and but little, both men and women'.

The latter wore 'a cloth about them from their middle to their knee and all the rest bare'.[10] The houses were 'very little, made of the branches of the palmer or coco-tree, and covered with the leaves of the same tree'.[11] There were, Fitch was told, 'no horses in all the country',[12] which was not in fact true. The elephants were 'not as great as those of Pegu, which be monstrous huge, but they say all other elephants do fear them and none dare fight them, though they be very small'.[13] The Portuguese exported elephants to their settlements on the west coast of India and used them for heavy work at arsenals and dockyards.

With his vessel provisioned and fresh water aboard, Fitch said goodbye to Ceylon, that 'brave island, very fruitful and fair, but [where] by reason of its continuous wars with the king thereof all things are very dear',[14] and prepared himself for the dangers of landing at Cochin. The ship doubled Cape Comorin, and Fitch noted that 'between Ceylon and the mainland . . . they fish for pearls. And there is fished every year very much, which doth serve all India.'[15] These pearl fisheries were famous throughout Asia, though the pearls were not considered to be as fine as those from Bahrein in the Persian Gulf. The fishing season was very short, barely a month between the middle of March and April.

When the season was approaching, between four and five thousand boats of various sizes assembled off the oyster beds, each with ten or twelve sailors and eight or nine divers. The divers could go down to great depths and were sometimes assumed to have magical protection against the sharks which infested the area. The merchants who had financed the divers would send out three ships to examine the beds, each team bringing back about a thousand oysters. These were then opened and examined and, depending on the quality of the pearls found, an offer was made to the king for the right to fish. When the offer was accepted, the king supplied a number of warships to protect the fishers against pirates.

The season was opened by the firing of a gun from one of the warships, and the fishing boats would then leave shore for the oyster beds. Each day the oysters collected would be placed on the sand, each merchant having his own enclosed space. The oysters were left to rot before opening. The season ended on 20 April but the sorting and sale of the pearls would go on for another fifty days, during which the enclosures had to be thoroughly cleaned. As a later traveller put it: 'So many flies are bred by the corrupt matter that the adjacent places and the whole country might be annoyed by them, if care were not taken to sweep into the sea the impurities collected during the fishery.'[16]

The fair itself was an important trading occasion. Merchants came from many parts of Asia and the Near East for the pearl sales. They brought with them other merchandise—fine jewellery, Persian carpets, gold bars, and fine cloth from India. A sideline for the divers consisted of pieces of amber and coral, for which there was considerable demand.

Fitch did not see the pearl fishery for himself, even though it was the season when his ship passed on its way to Cochin. His vessel was presumably carrying a specific cargo for Cochin and nowhere else, for it did not even put in to the important town of Quilon, 'from whence cometh great store of pepper'.[17] On 22 March 1589, Fitch arrived at Cochin. Two days earlier, a vessel had left for the Persian Gulf. There was nothing for Fitch to do except stay at Cochin in the hope that another ship would arrive. He waited eight months.

During his stay—of which, characteristically, he gives no

details—Fitch collected information about the Malabar coast and other parts of southern India. He was now in the heart of the Portuguese enterprise in India. Further up the coast, at Calicut, Vasco da Gama had landed in 1498. At that time, Cochin was a small principality owing allegiance to the ruler of Calicut, and when the Portuguese began to explore the coast they were welcomed as possible allies. The Portuguese, then only in light strength in the Indian seas, were unable to help the ruler but were quick to see the advantages of an alliance. The most important factor was the weakness of the raja of Cochin, which promised to permit the Portuguese—when they were ready—to seize control of his country. The harbour of Cochin, too, unlike that of Calicut, offered considerable strategic advantages, for it could be easily defended from the sea. Cochin is a small island separated from the mainland by a maze of backwaters, and artillery mounted in ships could dominate the approaches against a land-based power.

To these major advantages was added another. Cochin was in the centre of Malabar, 'the great pepper country'. If the Portuguese could divert the trade from Calicut to Cochin, one of the reasons for the Portuguese presence in Asia would be satisfied. Success took some years, for the Portuguese were not unopposed. The ruler of Calicut, though a Hindu, was anxious to support the Muslim merchants on whom his profits depended. In 1500 he chased away a Portuguese fleet, but it was a Pyrrhic victory. The Portuguese returned, again under the command of Vasco da Gama who had volunteered to chastise the ruler of Calicut and demonstrate once and for all the extent of Portuguese power. Da Gama attacked ships and seized their cargoes. The captured vessels were then set on fire with their crews aboard. At Calicut the Portuguese ships opened fire on the town, vessels carrying rice and other commodities were plundered and their crews mutilated. A Brahmin envoy of the ruler, who had arrived under a pledge of safe conduct, had his ears, nose and hands cut off, and was sent back to his master with them strung round his neck. Accompanying him was a letter from da Gama suggesting to the ruler that he 'have a curry made to eat of what the [Brahmin] brought him'.[18]

Naturally enough, this piece of wanton brutality, instead of intimidating the ruler, only increased his bellicosity. Da Gama was forced to raise his siege of Calicut. He sailed away to Cochin where he was sure of a welcome, especially with so large and heavily armed a fleet. But the raja soon discovered that, instead of an ally, he had found a new master. Da Gama demanded the right to construct a fort, and though the raja agreed he received nothing in return, not even protection. Da Gama's ships had been loading pepper, cardamoms and other spices, and he was anxious to get back to Lisbon. The Cochin raja was left to the mercy of the ruler of Calicut.

During da Gama's stay at Cochin he was approached by a number of local Christians. The Church of Malabar was believed by its members to have been founded by the Apostle Thomas. The Malabar Christians thought that they had something in common with the Portuguese, who were Christians too, and offered their help and allegiance to the king of Portugal. Later, they were to find that the Portuguese considered them only as heretics, material for the persecution, brutality and fire of the Inquisition.

The Portuguese returned to the Malabar coast, drove off the garrison the ruler of Calicut had established at Cochin after his defeat of the abandoned raja, and began the construction of a fort. From this date, 1503, onwards, the Portuguese slowly established themselves on land. Local chiefs were attacked and made to pay homage to the raja of Cochin. The ships of the ruler of Calicut were attacked and destroyed. But for all their successes, the Portuguese could not dominate the local powers either at sea or on the land. It was obvious, however, that they were not to be driven away. The running war with the ruler of Calicut and his changing allies continued for some years, but the Portuguese finally decided that there was less profit in conquest than in alliance and, ultimately, control. A treaty was negotiated with the ruler of Calicut, and the Portuguese, instead of making their Indian headquarters at Cochin, settled at Goa instead. Afterwards they concentrated on attempting to impose their will through the possession of a few forts, intrigue, bribery, selective interference in the affairs of potential enemies and friends, and the use of sea power.

This policy was both bloody and varying in success. In 1540 a treaty was signed between the Portuguese and the ruler of Calicut, which gave them some ten years of peace if not friendship. But fighting broke out again. The Portuguese were attacked at sea by the Calicut admiral, Kunjali Marakkar. Though he might be defeated in one engagement he always appeared again, and sometimes was the victor. The ruler of Calicut attacked Portuguese forts on land and had a notable success at Chaliyam. By the time Fitch arrived at Cochin, the Portuguese had given up their attempts to dominate Calicut and the hinterland. They were still fighting occasional skirmishes on land, but the main action remained at sea, where Kunjali, whom the Portuguese insisted on calling a pirate, constantly attacked Portuguese vessels and interrupted their trade.

Fitch alleges that the ruler of Calicut always denied that he had any control over Kunjali, and in fact the admiral and his successors grew more and more independent of the ruler's authority. 'When the Portugals complain to the king', wrote Fitch, 'he saith he doth not send them out; but he consenteth that they go. They range all the coast from Ceylon to Goa, and go by four or five . . . boats together, and have in every one of them, fifty or threescore men . . . They do much harm on that coast and take every year many . . . boats of the Portugals.'[19] In the end, it was an alliance between the ruler of Calicut and the Portuguese which put an end to the Kunjalis in 1599.

After nearly a century of activity on the Malabar coast, the Portuguese political achievement was limited; they still controlled only their puppet raja of Cochin, and were in alliance with the rulers of Cannanore, Quilon and one or two other minor princes. The raja of Cochin, whose territories covered only a few miles outside the Portuguese fort, was virtually a prisoner. Fitch saw him travelling in his enclosed palanquin—'incached', is the word he uses. The raja, who had little else to do, spent most of his time moving from one of his 'palaces' to another. Fitch remarks that he 'hath many houses, but they be but little. His guard is small.'[20] All of which befitted a puppet.

The other inhabitants of Cochin also had little houses, 'covered with the leaves of the coco-trees. The men be of reasonable stature, the women little; all black with a cloth bound about their middle hanging down to their hams; all the rest of their bodies are naked.'[21] Fitch noted, as other travellers had done before, that the people of Cochin had 'horrible great ears with many rings set in pearls and stones in them'.[22] Federici, who was there some thirty years earlier, was given permission to measure the 'circumference of one of them [the ears] with a thread', and found that it was the length of his arm. 'They do make them', he said, 'when they be little, for then they open the ear, and hang a piece of gold or lead thereat, and within the opening they put a certain leaf that they have for that purpose, which maketh the whole so great.'[23]

But the main interest for Fitch, that very commercial traveller, was the pepper trade. 'Here groweth the pepper', he wrote, 'and it springeth up by a tree or a pole and like our ivy-berry, but something longer, like the wheat-ear . . . It doth grow in the fields among the bushes without any labour . . . When they first gather it it is green, and then they lay it in the Sun and it becometh black.'[24]

Despite the almost continuous conflict on land and sea between the Portuguese and local rulers, merchants and their foreign allies, it was the pepper trade of the Malabar coast that the Portuguese found profitable. Though their leaders often pretended that they were doing Christ's work in Asia, it was fortunate that the heathen also indulged in trade. God and Mammon could be satisfied at the same time. But the religious aspect was essentially a side issue. The Portuguese fought to obtain control of the spice trade, and to a large extent they succeeded. By various methods—bribery and coercion among them—they increased the pepper output of Malabar and carried it away in their own ships to the Near East and Europe.

It was not entirely a one-way passage. The Portuguese encouraged inter-Asian trade and expanded it, to their profit, but they also introduced new crops into Malabar and found new uses and markets for such traditional ones as the coconut. They discovered that coir made fine ropes. From this the Portuguese made their rigging, having discovered that it did not rot in salt water. 'All the ships are caulked with it,' too, wrote Garcia da Orta, 'so that it serves as linen, as oakum and as matting. These qualities', he added, 'make it good merchandise for Portugal.'[25] This was the foundation of a trade in a product which is still one of the principal exports of Malabar.

With all their preoccupations, the Portuguese had found time to make of Cochin a splendid small city instead of the village they had found on their arrival. As usual, there were a number of churches and religious foundations. Most travellers agreed that the Jesuit church was the finest of the buildings. The fort was considered one of the strongest in that part of India.

With the passing months, Fitch's position must have been continually precarious. No doubt he had acquaintances among the Portuguese with whom he stayed. It is unlikely that they took him for an Englishman, for if they had he would probably have been arrested. Now, it was not only Fitch himself who was wanted by the authorities. England and Spain were at war, and every Englishman was an enemy. Under the circumstances, it is all the more surprising that Fitch should have been prepared to risk a visit to Goa itself. Perhaps there was no alternative. When a ship on which he could embark arrived at Cochin, it was more than likely that it would put in to Goa at one stage of the voyage.

On 2 November 1589, Fitch left Cochin on a Portuguese ship which stayed at Goa for three days. The next stage was Chaul, where he was forced to remain for twenty-three days, either while the same vessel loaded cargo, or while he waited for another one to carry him—he does not say. From Chaul he sailed to Ormuz, another dangerous place for him, especially as he was unlucky enough to have to wait fifty days there for a passage to Basra. Again, he gives no details, leaving the questions of where he stayed, what he pretended to be, whether he was ever under suspicion, unanswered.

It is typical of Fitch that, even now on his journey home with valuable information for his employers—who had not heard from him for years—he should be looking for new experiences and new places to visit. After escaping from the threat of the Portuguese at Ormuz, he followed the usual route by retracing his steps from Basra to Baghdad. But from there, instead of taking the shortest way to Tripoli, where he hoped to find an English ship to take him home, he made a diversion and visited some of the trading centres of Asia Minor.

On his way out to India, Fitch and his party had travelled down the Euphrates river from the caravan station at Birejik to Baghdad. Now, from Baghdad, Fitch was to make for Birejik by way of the river Tigris, or, rather, by the caravan route that roughly followed the course of that river. His first important stopping place was the trading centre of Mosul, 'which standeth near to Nineveh, which is all ruinated and destroyed'.[26] From Mosul, he went on to Mardin in the highlands of Kurdistan, which was then an important junction on the caravan road from Baghdad. At Mardin, the northern fork led to Constantinople, but Fitch—making first for Aleppo, where he knew he would find English friends—turned south and came to Urfa.

Urfa was 'a very fair town (and it hath a goodly fountain full of fish), where the Moors hold many great ceremonies and opinions concerning Abraham'.[27] Urfa was an important place of pilgrimage, for it contained both the cradle and the tomb of Abraham, or so the Muslims believed. Fitch was unable to see the holy place, for Christians were not allowed near it. Fitch's 'goodly fountain of fish' was the Pool of Abraham, a great rock pool fed by a spring, in which swam Abraham's carp.

Once again Fitch passed the river Euphrates at Birejik and arrived at Aleppo, where he 'stayed certain months for company',[28] glad, without doubt, to find Englishmen to talk to about his adventures and the state of the world he had been so long away from. Though he does not give a date, it was probably January 1591, and he stayed at Aleppo not for a few months but only for a few weeks. From Aleppo he made his way to Tripoli, 'where finding English shipping, I came with a prosperous voyage to London, where by God's assistance I safely arrived the 29th of April 1591, having been eight years out of my native country'.[29]

X

Charter for empire

The England Fitch returned to after his lengthy travels was one especially anxious and ready to be stimulated by what he had to say about the riches and the potentialities of trade in the East Indies. In 1588 the English had defeated the Spanish Armada, destroying once and for all the menace of Spain. This victory in itself released the fears and tensions which had, to a significant extent, inhibited English merchants from investing in the hazards of seaborne enterprise. The seas were now clear, and the English did not need to fear the journey around the Cape of Good Hope to India. This did not mean that the land route followed by Fitch and his companions was automatically ruled out. On the contrary, the merchants of the Levant Company wanted the monopoly of that route for themselves.

The charter of the Company was due for renewal, and there could be no better person to put to the queen the case for an extension of the old rights of trade than the first Englishman to travel in India and reach the gateway to China. There was certainly no one better qualified. It is obvious that, if John Newbery had survived, he would already have reported on the party's experience at the court of the Great Mogul and would have been closely involved in the negotiations over the new charter. No doubt Fitch enquired, wherever he could, on his journey home.

The mystery of Newbery's fate is made more opaque by the fact that his name is never mentioned except by Samuel Purchas in his collection of travels, who gives the impression that Newbery actually reached England. But there is little doubt that Newbery died some time after he left Lahore. Of the party he had inspired and led, only Ralph Fitch returned to London. It was to Fitch, therefore, that the governors of the Levant Company turned, and an 'ample relation of his wonderful travailes' was sent to the queen's chief secretary and most influential adviser, Lord Burghley.

It seems improbable that this 'ample relation' was identical with the version of Fitch's travels published later by Richard Hakluyt in his collection of *The Principal Navigations Voyages Traffiques and Discoveries of the English Nation* (1598–1600). It probably contained more detail of the trade and products of the East Indies than Hakluyt included in the printed version, although there, in his last pages, Fitch catalogues some of the products 'which India and the country further Eastward do bring forth'.[1] As well as the pepper of the coast of Malabar, Fitch reported that ginger grew there 'like unto our garlic'.[2] Cloves—'their tree is like to our bay tree'[3]—came from the Moluccas, and nutmegs and mace from the island of Banda; 'their tree is like to our walnut-tree but somewhat lesser'.[4] From the island of Timor came white sandalwood, 'very sweet and in great request among the Indians, for they grind it with a little water and anoint their bodies therewith'.[5]

Among the other exotic products Fitch mentions is camphor, 'a precious thing amongst the Indians and is sold dearer than gold'.[6] He reported that some came from China, but that the best was found in the island of Borneo, where it 'groweth in canes'.[7] This last was an error. In fact, Bornean camphor came from a very large tree, but was packed for export inside hollow bamboo. From 'Cauchinchina' (Cochin China) came 'lignum aloes'. Sometimes called 'eagle-wood'—a complicated corruption of the original Sanskrit name—it was once greatly prized in Europe as incense.

Another variety of incense was 'benjamin' or benzoin, which came from Siam or Java and was sometimes called Java frankincense. Fitch's list continues with 'long pepper', musk, amber, rubies, sapphires and diamonds, and pearls concerning which he mentions Hainan, 'a great Island on the Southermost coast of China' as one of the sources.[8] From Cambodia, among other strange drugs came 'spodium', a substance frequently referred to by travellers of the time (and earlier) but for which there is no simple definition. It is usually taken to mean the product of burnt vegetable matter or bone, such as ivory-black.

In his printed narrative, Fitch does not mention details of one of the most interesting items in the East's exotic merchandise—the bezoar stone. This was thought to be an antidote for poisons of one kind or another. The bezoars were actually solid concretions found in the alimentary canal of ruminant mammals, and in the Indian pharmacopoeia had different names according to which animal they came from. The bezoar was sometimes called a snake stone, because it was thought to come from the head of a snake, but this was an error arising from the fact that a bezoar stone was regarded as being an antidote for snake bite. According to some travellers, the stone was also a remedy for cholera, and one claimed that it was efficacious 'for the ailments of women's wombs and thus for malign fevers . . . for all these evils it is applied by being placed in ordinary water. Being left there for two Credos, it gives the water a bitter taste, so that when it be drunk it improves the patients admirably. This stone improperly so called . . . is like unto a ball of soap, being soft. And it is consumed if it is left in water. Most of these stones are of a dark yellow colour and a bitterish flavour, which one feels immediately upon touching one of them with the tip of one's tongue.'[9]

Obviously, Fitch's 'relation' helped to influence Lord Burghley, for on 7 January 1592 a charter was granted to 'the Governor and Company of Merchants of the Levant', with Sir Edward Osborne as the first governor. In the charter, Ralph Fitch was listed among the members. The charter was to run for twelve years, and the area of activity was now expanded from the Turkish dominions of the previous grant to include those of the Venetian republic and, more significantly, the trade 'by land through the countries of the said Grand Signor [the sultan of Turkey] into and from the East Indies, lately discovered' by Fitch and his companions.[10]

It seems probable that the new Company considered the overland route to India as still a working proposition, though it might be thought that Fitch's experiences would have convinced them otherwise. Perhaps Fitch himself believed such a route might be made commercially viable—and this may have been the reason why he himself returned to the Levant. When he left is not known, but he was certainly there in 1596. In that year, the English merchants of the Levant Company at Aleppo elected Fitch as their consul, and wrote to the Company's representative at Constantinople to report that 'the whole company of merchants here resident with one assent and consent have elected Master Ralph Fitch our absolute consul'.[11] This was unfortunately taken by the Company in London as an attempt by its employees to dictate policy. The merchants at Aleppo had refused to accept the Company's own nominee for consul and had taken matters into their own hands by appointing Fitch. This the Company would not tolerate, and wrote to its agent at Constantinople saying that 'though the company [i.e. the merchants] there at Aleppo have appointed one Master Fitch (a sufficient man), yet, because our orders is that the consul must be made here [London] and here take his oath and enter into bond for the true and upright using himself in his office',[12] Fitch could not be confirmed in his appointment.

The next heard of Fitch is that, according to Hakluyt, he was 'living here in London'. This was about 1599. It was the right time for him to be back in England, for new views about the East India trade were about to be given form. Nineteen days before Fitch's return to London in 1591, an expedition had sailed from Plymouth for the East Indies. The little fleet of three ships had been badly equipped, and suffered in consequence, only one actually reaching the eastern seas. This ship, the *Edward Bonaventure*, commanded by James Lancaster, at least proved that the journey by the Cape of Good Hope was possible, though on its return the ship was blown aground on an island in the Gulf of Mexico, where Lancaster had gone in search of further profit. The results could only be assessed in terms of experience.

But it was that experience, however disastrous, of the eastern seas which, together with the store of facts built up from the narratives of travellers, suggested that enough was known to make English merchants consider that the time was ripe for a commercial expedition to the East Indies. In trade, the best stimulus to activity is competition. In 1597 news reached England that the Dutch were already proving the feasibility of breaking the Portuguese monopoly in the commerce of Asia. At the beginning of 1595 a fleet had left Holland and returned home two years later richly loaded with spices and other exotic products. If the Dutch could do it, so could the English, especially as the English would be forced to continue buying their spices from the Dutch if they did not break into the trade themselves.

This, in fact, is just what happened. The Dutch quickly settled themselves into the spice trade at its point of origin and charged their customers whatever price they thought the market would stand. There seemed to be miserable prospects for the future if nothing was done, and a number of English merchants, including some who were already associated with the Levant Company and were most active in bringing it about, held a meeting. The date was 24 September 1599. Two days earlier a list of investors had been opened. Among the hundred and one 'persons as have written with their own hands, to venture in the pretended voyage to the East Indies (the which it may please the Lord to prosper)'[13] was John Eldred, committed for the sum of £400.

Ralph Fitch was not among the subscribers, nor was he present at the meeting. It is probable that he did not have the capital available for investment, but there is no doubt that he was well known to those who had, and had been consulted before the decision to call a meeting was taken. At the meeting, at which eighty of the subscribers were present, it was decided to petition the queen for her royal assent to a project 'intended for the honour of their native country and the advancement of trade and merchandise within the realm of England . . . to set forth a voyage to the East Indies and other islands and countries thereabouts'.[14]

Naturally, the subscribers wanted to get their ships away as quickly as possible. On 16 October there was another meeting at which it was disclosed that the queen was prepared to give her assent, but that something was holding up the formal granting of permission. That something was the prospect of peace with Spain. Philip II was dead, and his successor had opened up negotiations. Fearing that a voyage to the East Indies might upset these, the queen and her Privy Council were unwilling to give permission. The subscribers therefore provided a lengthy memorial with the title: 'Certain Reasons why the English Merchants may trade into the East Indies, especially to such rich Kingdoms and Dominions as are not subject to the King of Spain and Portugal; together with the true limits of the Portugals' conquest and jurisdiction in those Oriental parts'. This document was in effect a summary of all that had been gathered together about the Spanish and Portuguese possessions overseas and those countries with which the merchants hoped to trade. It ended with the statement that 'in all these and infinite places more, abounding with great wealth and riches, the Portugals and Spaniards have not any castle, fort, blockhouse, or commandment'.[15] Included in the evidence cited in support was 'Mr Ralph Fitch's Travels through most of the Portugal Indies'.

The facts collected in this document, and the lobbying of interested parties, finally produced the queen's assent to the project of a voyage to the East Indies. But it took time. In September 1600 another meeting of subscribers was held, at which it was made clear that the formal permission would be sent soon and that ships must be bought and cargoes arranged. James Lancaster was to command the fleet, and at another meeting held on 2 October it was 'ordered that . . . Master Eldred and Master Fitch shall in the meeting tomorrow morning confer of the merchandise fit to be provided for the first voyage'.[16]

The advice of Eldred and Fitch was not recorded, but the cargo decided upon for the first voyage appears in the Court Minutes for 8 October 1600.[17]

		£ s d
Iron	tons 30 at	270 00 00
Tin wrought	tons 5	330 00 00
Tin unwrought in bars	tons 5	420 00 00
Lead	tons 100	1700 00 00
Cloths 80 of these sorts viz.		
2 scarlets in 4 halves		
4 stammells*		
8 blues		
8 Azures		
8 Plunketts†		
8 Popinjays‡		
4 grass greens		
8 sad greens		
8 venice greens		
4 olive colours		
8 Reading cloths mingled 2 of each colour		
2 hair colours		
4 violet		
4 primrose colours		
80	at £16 per cloth per estimate	1280 00 00
Devonshire kerseys of like colours 80 pieces		200 00 00
hamshires of all colours 20 pieces at £3 10s		65 00 00
Norwich stuff 100 at discretion		250 00 00

*A kind of woollen stuff dyed red.
†A woollen cloth, usually bright blue in colour, but sometimes crimson.
‡A brightly coloured red or green woollen cloth made in Gloucester.

In addition to the merchandise, there was to be a 'present to be given to the king' of the country where the fleet was to make its landfall. This consisted of:

A Belt or Girdle
A Case of Pistols
Some Plumes
Looking glasses
Platters, spoons and toys of glass
Spectacles and Drinking glasses of all sorts
An Ewer of plain Silver

With the cost of the present at £30, the total value of the cargo was £4545. It was hoped that it could be sold or exchanged for spices and other goods. Fitch would have informed the merchants of the kind of goods the Portuguese used in their trade. The iron and tin would probably find a ready market, but it must have seemed to him that the broadcloth for which England was so famous in Europe would be no more than an exotic novelty to the rulers of the East Indies. Broadcloth, however, was the commodity England had to export, and those who had put up the money for the venture would have to be convinced—by experience if necessary—that it would not sell. Wisely, the subscribers took at least part of Fitch's advice and decided to send with the fleet a large quantity of bullion. Permission was granted to send £30,000 in specie, but £6000 of this, it was insisted, had to be in coin bearing the head of Elizabeth. This was to turn out to be something of a disadvantage. The accepted and acceptable currency of the East Indies was that of Portugal and Spain, and English money was found to be of little value.

By the end of the year 1600—on, in fact, the last day of the century—the merchants received their long-awaited Charter from the queen. It was a very long and prolix document, heavy with the characteristic tautology of Elizabethan official English. After the queen's titles, it addressed 'all our officers, ministers, and subjects and . . . all other people, as well within our realm of England as elsewhere' and noted that 218 named individuals had 'been petitioners unto us for our royal assent and license' so that they, 'at their own adventure, costs and charges, as well as for the honour of our realm of England, as for the increase of our navigation, and advancement of trade of merchandise, within our said realm, and the dominions of the same, might adventure and set forth one or more voyages, with convenient number of ships and pinnaces, by way of traffic and merchandise to the East Indies, in the countries and parts of Asia and Africa, and to as many of the islands, ports and cities, towns and places, thereabouts, as where trade and traffic may by all likelihood be discovered, established or had; divers of which countries, and many of the islands, cities and ports thereof, have long since been discovered by others of our subjects, albeit not frequented in trade of merchandise'.

In accordance with this petition, her majesty, 'greatly tendering the honour of our nation, the wealth of our people, and the encouragement of them, and others of our loving subjects in their good enterprises, for the increase of our navigation, and the advancement of lawful traffic, to the benefit of our commonwealth', constituted the petitioners a 'body corporate and politick, in deed and in name, by the name of *The Governor and Company of the Merchants of London, trading into the East Indies*'.

The area allotted to the Company was vast—'all the islands, ports, havens, cities, creeks, towns and places of Asia, Africa, and America, or any of them beyond the Cape of Bona Esperanza to the Straits of Magellan, where any trade or traffic or merchandise may be used or had'. The charter gave to a small body of merchants an exclusive monopoly of Asian trade, and all other men, 'of what degree or quality soever they be', were strictly forbidden to trade in any area allotted to the Company. Anyone defying this prohibition would 'incur our indignation, and the forfeiture and loss of the goods, merchandises and other things whatsoever, which so shall be brought into this realm of England'.[18] The culprits' ships, too, would be seized and the profits divided equally between the Crown and the Company.

It was, in effect, a charter for empire, though it is highly unlikely that either the queen or the merchants of the new Company considered it as such.

Captain Lancaster's little fleet left Woolwich on 13 February 1601, eighteen years almost to the day after Fitch and his companions had set out on their journey to India. Lancaster, however, was not making for India at all, but for the island of Sumatra and the territories of Portugal's greatest enemy in the eastern seas, the ruler of Acheh. Perhaps Fitch's report on the extent of Portuguese power in India itself, and his and other travellers' information on the Spice Islands, had convinced the Company that their first voyage should be made with as little avoidable risk as possible. In any case, it was reasonable to assume that such a determined enemy of the Portuguese as the ruler of Acheh would welcome the appearance of another European nation as a possible ally.

Lancaster was, in fact, very well received a few days after his arrival in June 1602. He had been thoughtfully provided with a number of copies, suitably sealed, of a letter from Queen Elizabeth, with blanks left to be filled in with the name of the appropriate recipient. The ruler of Acheh received one of these with interest, if not with comprehension. Lancaster met with no opposition from the Dutch merchants already well established there, but there were some intrigues on the part of the Portuguese despite the fact that the Achinese ruler prevented news of Lancaster's arrival from reaching Malacca. But Lancaster's main purpose—to purchase a cargo of spices—could not be satisfied at Acheh, where stocks were low. He therefore sailed on to Bantam in Java. There one of the queen's letters was again favourably received and permission was granted for the English to establish an agency.

After an adventurous journey, Lancaster arrived back in England on 11 September 1603 with a cargo of over a million pounds of pepper. This triumphant homecoming, with its proof that the English could hope to profit from the spice trade, was somewhat tarnished by an order from the new king, James I, that the cargo could not be sold until his own private stocks of spices—captured from a Portuguese carrack—had been disposed of. It seemed at first as if the bright vision of a company of merchants of London trading to the East Indies was to dissolve in debts and bankruptcy. Fortunately, the king relented, the Company's pepper reached the market, and the subscribers began to prepare for a second voyage. This set out in March 1604, again to the ports of Java and Sumatra.

While a third voyage was in preparation, the Treaty of London (August 1604) was signed with the united kingdom of Spain and Portugal, and this raised hopes that the Portuguese would not interfere with English attempts to trade in the dominions of the Great Mogul. The Court Minutes of the Company are missing for the period between August 1603 and December 1606, so the trend of the subscribers' thinking is not known. There must, however, have been many discussions, and it is reasonable to assume that Ralph Fitch was again appealed to for information and advice. Certainly, by December 1606 it had been decided that, on the next voyage to Bantam, the fleet should make for the island of Socotra, there to pick up a pilot and—if the weather permitted—visit Aden. If sufficient cargo could be loaded there, one of the ships was to be sent home while the other two went on to Bantam, calling, if possible, at the coast of Gujarat to enquire into the possibility of 'a maintenance of trade in those parts hereafter in safety from the danger of the Portugals or other enemies, endeavouring also to learn whether the King of Cambay or Surat or any of his havens be in subjection to the Portugals, and what havens of his are not'.[19]

The commander, William Hawkins, was to be prepared to visit the rulers if he could, and the Court Minutes of 31 December 1606 record that 'it is further ordered that letters be provided by this Company from his Majesty to be sent to the King of Cambay, and the Governor of Aden and to 2 places more not far from Aden, what titles to give them is to be inquired of Ralph Fitch'.[20] The letters were provided and Hawkins did call at Surat—his vessel, the first to show the English flag in those waters, anchoring in the mouth of the river on which the town stands on 24 August 1608. The English were off on the dangerous and bloody road that was to lead to their conquest of the whole of India.

The entry in the Court Minutes of 1606 is the last mention of Ralph Fitch in the records of the Company he did so much to help bring into being. Of the rest of his life, nothing is known. It is possible that two wills lodged at Somerset House in London, in which the testator is named as Ralph Fitch, citizen and leather-seller of London, are those of the first Englishman to reach the heart of India. The first is dated 14 February 1583 and was proved in February 1590, presumably on the assumption that the testator was dead. It must have been something of a surprise to his executors when he turned up in the following year. The wills are certainly those of the same person, for both mention a brother Thomas, a sister Frances, and a niece of the same name—but neither wife nor child. The second will was made on 3 October 1616 and proved on 15 October of the same year, indicating that Fitch died between those two dates. The year before, a courtier, Sir Thomas Roe, had arrived in the capital of the Great Mogul as the ambassador of the

Company and of King James, intent on proving to the son and successor of the emperor Fitch had seen thirty years before that the English 'were not all obsequious merchants or rough sailors'. After the pioneer had come the diplomat.

Appendix

Ralph Fitch: his itinerary 1583/91

Depart	*Arrive*
London 12 February 1583	Gravesend 12 February 1583
Gravesend 13 February	The Downs, off Deal, 25 February
Deal 25 February	Falmouth 11 March
Falmouth 11 March	Tripoli 1 May
Tripoli 14 May	Hamah 17 May (?)
Hamah 17 May (?)	Aleppo 21 May
Aleppo 31 May	Birejik 2 June
Birejik 2 June	Fellujah 28 June
Fellujah 5 July (?)	Baghdad 6 July (?)
Baghdad 27 July	Basra 6 August

Eldred leaves. Newbery, Fitch, Story, Leedes, continue journey

Depart	Arrive
Basra 20 August (?)	Ormuz 4 September
Ormuz 11 October	Diu 5 November
Diu 5 November (?)	Daman 7 November (?)
Bassein 9 November (?)	Thana 9 November (?)
Thana 9 November (?)	Chaul 10 November
Chaul 20 November (?)	Goa 29 November

Story remains in Goa. Newbery, Fitch, and Leedes continue journey

Depart	Arrive
Goa 5 April 1585	Belgaum April 1585 (?)
Belgaum April 1585 (?)	Bijapur April 1585 (?)
Bijapur April (?)	Golconda April (?)
Golconda May (?)	Bidar May (?)
Bidar May (?)	Balapur May (?)
Balapur (May (?)	Burhanpur May (?)
Burhanpur May (?)	Mandu June (?)
Mandu June (?)	Ujjain June (?)
Ujjain June (?)	Sironj June (?)

Depart	*Arrive*
Sironj June (?)	Agra July (?)
Agra July (?)	Fatehpur Sikri July (?)
Newbery leaves for home, Leedes takes service with Akbar, Fitch continues journey	
Fatehpur Sikri October (?)	Agra October 1585 (?)
Agra October (?)	Allahabad November (?)
Allahabad November (?)	Banaras December (?)
Banaras December (?)	Patna January 1586 (?)
Patna January 1586 (?)	Tanda February 1586 (?)
Tanda February (?)	Cooch Behar March(?)
Cooch Behar March (?)	Hugli April (?)
Hugli May (?)	Satgaon May (?)
Satgaon July (?)	Chittagong August (?)
Chittagong August (?)	Barisal September (?)
Barisal September (?)	Sripur October (?)
Sripur 28 November 1586	Negrais 5 December (?)
Negrais 6 December (?)	Bassein (Burma) 9 December (?)
Bassein (Burma) 9 December (?)	Myaungmya 10 December (?)
Myaungmya 10 December (?)	Dala 11 December (?)
Dala 12 December (?)	Syriam 14 December (?)
Syriam 15 December (?)	Mayet-kyi 15 December (?)
Mayet-kyi 16 December (?)	Pegu 16 December (?)
Pegu (?)	Chiengmai (Thailand) (?)
Chiengmai (Thailand) (?)	Pegu (?)
Pegu 10 January (?) 1587	Malacca 8 February (?) 1587
Malacca 29 March 1588	Bassein (Burma) 24 September 1588 (?)
Bassein (Burma) October (?)	Bengal November (?)
Bengal 3 February 1589	Ceylon 6 March 1589
Ceylon 11 March	Cochin 22 March
Cochin 2 November	Goa 10 November (?)
Goa 13 November (?)	Chaul 18 November (?)
Chaul 11 December (?)	Ormuz 7 January 1590 (?)
Ormuz 26 February 1590 (?)	Basra 20 March (?)
Basra (?)	Baghdad (?)
Baghdad (?)	Mosul (?)
Mosul (?)	Mardin (?)
Mardin (?)	Urfah (?)
Urfah (?)	Birejik (?)
Birejik January 1591 (?)	Aleppo January 1591 (?)
Aleppo January 1591 (?)	Tripoli February 1591 (?)
Tripoli 12 February 1591 (?)	London 29 April 1591

Bibliography

ABUL FAZL ALLAMI. *Ain-i-Akbari*. Trs. H. Blochman and H. S. Jarrett. 3 vols. Calcutta 1873, 1891, 1894

BARBOSA. *The Book of Duarte Barbosa*. Trs. Longworth Dames. 2 vols. London 1918, 1921

BARROS and COUTO. *Da Asia de Joao de Barros e de Diogo de Couto*. 24 vols. Lisbon 1778

BARTOLI, D. *Missione al Grand Mogor de Padre Ridolfo Aquaviva*. 5th edn. Rome 1714

BERNIER, F. *Travels in the Mogul Empire*. Trs. A. Constable, ed. V. A. Smith. London 1914

BEVERIDGE, H. *A Comprehensive History of India*. London n.d.

BIRDWOOD, Sir G. *The Register of Letters &tc. of the Governour and Company of Merchants of London Trading to the East Indies*. London 1893

BOXER, C. R. *Fidalgos in the Far East 1550–1770*. The Hague 1948

CARLETTI, F. *My Voyage around the World*. Trs. H. Weinstock. London 1965

DANVERS, F. C. *The Portuguese in India*. 2 vols. London 1894

DELLON, Dr. C. *Relation de l'Inquisition à Goa*. Paris 1688

ELLIOT, H. M., and DOWSON, J. *The History of India as told by its own Historians*. Vol. VI. London 1875

D'EREDIA, G. 'Description of Malacca', in *Journal of the Royal Asiatic Society, Malayan Branch*. Vol. VIII pt. 1. Kuala Lumpur 1930

FONSECA, J. N. *An Historical and Archaeological Sketch of the City of Goa*. Bombay 1878

FOSTER, W. *Early Travels in India 1583–1619*. London 1921

DA GAMA *The Three Voyages of Vasco da Gama*. Trs., from the *Lendas da India* of Gaspar Correa, by Lord Stanley of Alderley. London 1869

HAKLUYT, R. *The Principal Navigations, Voyages, Traffiques and Discoveries of the English Nation* [1599.] 12 vols. Glasgow 1903–5

HARVEY, G. E. *History of Burma*. London 1925

Hmannan Yazawin. 3 vols. Mandalay 1908

DE LAET, J. *The Empire of the Great Mogul*. Trs. and ed. J. S. Hoyland and S. N. Banerjee. Bombay 1928

LINSCHOTEN. *The Voyage of John Huygen van Linschoten to the East Indies*. Ed. A. C. Burnell and P. A. Tiele. 2 vols. London 1884

LOCKE, J. C. *The First Englishmen in India*. London 1930

MACLAGAN, Sir E. *The Jesuits and the Great Mogul.* London 1932
MANRIQUE. *The Travels of Fray Sebastien Manrique.* Trs. C. E. Luard and H. Hosten. London 1926
MONSERRATE. *The Commentary of Father Monserrate S. J.* Ed. J. S. Hoyland and S. N. Banerjee. London 1922
MONTALTO DE JESUS, C. A. *Historic Macao.* Hongkong 1902
MORELAND, W. H. (1) *India at the Death of Akbar.* London 1920
MORELAND, W. H. (2) *Relations of Golconda in the Early Seventeenth Century.* London 1931
MORELAND, W. H. (3), and GEYL, P. *Jahangir's India: The Remonstratie of Francesco Pesaert.* Cambridge 1925
DA ORTA, GARCIA. *Colloquies on the Simples and Drugs of India.* Trs. Clements Markham. London 1913
PANIKKAR, K. M. *Malabar and the Portuguese.* Bombay 1929
PAYNE, C. H. (ed. and trs.) *Akbar and the Jesuits: An Account of the Jesuit Missions to the Court of Akbar by Father Pierre du Jarric S. J.* London 1926
PIERIS, P. E. *Ceylon: The Portuguese Era.* 2 vols. Colombo 1913
PINTO. *The Voyages and Adventures of Fernand Mendez Pinto.* Trs. (1653) H. Cogan, ed. H. Vambery. London 1891
PIRES. *The Summa Oriental of Tome Pires.* Trs. and ed. A. Cortesao. 2 vols. London 1944
POLO. *The Travels of Marco Polo.* Trs. R. Latham. London 1958
PRASAD, R. C. *Early English Travellers in India.* Delhi 1965
PURCHAS, S. *Hakluytus Postumus or Purchas his Pilgrimes.* [1625.] 20 vols. Glasgow 1905–7
PYRARD. *The Voyage of François Pyrard de Laval to the East Indies.* Trs. and ed. A. Gray and H. C. P. Bell. London 1889
REBEIRO, JOAO. *History of Ceylon.* Trs. G. Lee. Colombo 1847
RYLEY, J. H. *Ralph Fitch. England's Pioneer to India and Burma.* London 1899
SASTRI, K. A. NILAKANTA. *A History of South India.* 3rd edn. Madras 1966
SHIAB-UD-DIN TALISH *Fahiyyah-i-ibriyyah,* in the *Journal of the Asiatic Society of Bengal.* Calcutta. June 1907
SIMKIN, C. G. F. *The Traditional Trade of Asia.* London 1968
SMITH V. A. *Akbar the Great Mogul.* Oxford 1917
STEVENS, H., and BIRDWOOD, Sir G. *The Dawn of British Trade to the East Indies as recorded in the Court Minutes of the East India Company 1599–1603.* London 1886
WINDSTEDT, R. O. *A History of Malaya.* Singapore 1962
WOOD, A. *History of the Levant Company.* London 1935

Notes on sources

I In search of spices

1 Hakluyt, vol. v, pp. 192–202
2 ibid. pp. 450–51

II The road to Ormuz

1 Newbery, in Hakluyt, vol. v, p. 453
2 Eldred, in Locke, p. 34
3 ibid. p. 34
4 ibid. p. 36
5 ibid. p. 37
6 Newbery, in Hakluyt, vol. v, p. 454
7 ibid.
8 Fitch, in Hakluyt, vol. v, pp. 465—66
9 ibid. p. 466
10 ibid.
11 Eldred, in Locke, p. 44
12 ibid.
13 ibid. p. 45
14 Fitch, in Hakluyt, vol. v, pp. 466–67
15 Eldred, in Locke, p. 49
16 Newbery, in Locke, p. 51
17 ibid. p. 50
18 Newbery, in Hakluyt, vol. v, p. 462
19 Fitch, in Hakluyt, vol. v, p. 463
20 ibid.

III Golden Goa

1 Newbery, in Hakluyt, vol. v, p. 460
2 Fitch, in Hakluyt, vol. v, p. 469
3 Samuel Butler *Hudibras* (1674), part II, canto i
4 Fitch, in Hakluyt, vol. v, p. 470
5 ibid. p. 463
6 ibid. p. 464
7 Linschoten, in Hakluyt, vol. v, p. 508
8 ibid.
9 Fitch, in Hakluyt, vol. v, p. 464
10 Linschoten, in Hakluyt, vol. v, p. 509
11 Linschoten, in Fonseca, p. 198
12 Pyrard de Laval, vol. II, part iii, p. 66
13 Linschoten, in Purchas, vol. X, p. 234
14 Pyrard de Laval, vol. II, part iii, p. 69
15 ibid. p. 103
16 Dellon, p. 44
17 Linschoten, in Hakluyt, vol. v, p. 510
18 Fitch, in Hakluyt, vol. v, p. 472
19 Linschoten, in Hakluyt, vol. v, p. 511
20 ibid.

IV Diamonds and idolaters

1 Fitch, in Hakluyt, vol. v, p. 472
2 ibid.
3 Asad Beg *Wikaya-i,* in Elliot and Dowson, vol. vi, pp. 163–64
4 Fitch, in Hakluyt, vol. v, p. 472

5 ibid.
6 ibid.
7 ibid. p. 470
8 ibid. p. 471
9 Polo, p. 232
10 Fitch, in Hakluyt, vol. v, p. 472
11 Methwold, in Moreland (2), p. 9
12 ibid.
13 Fitch, in Hakluyt, vol. v, p. 472
14 Methwold, in Moreland (2), p. 17
15 ibid.
16 ibid. p. 18
17 ibid.
18 Fitch, in Hakluyt, vol. v, p. 472
19 ibid.
20 ibid.
21 ibid.
22 ibid. p. 473
23 ibid.
24 ibid.
25 ibid.
26 ibid.
27 ibid.
28 Fitch, in Hakluyt, vol. v, p. 470
29 Monserrate, p. 62
30 ibid.
31 Fitch, in Hakluyt, vol. v, p. 473
32 ibid.
33 Monserrate, p. 20
34 ibid. p. 21
35 Fitch, in Hakluyt, vol. v, p. 473
36 ibid.

V The court of the Great Mogul

1 Fitch, in Hakluyt, vol. v, p. 474
2 ibid.
3 Abul Fazl *Ain-i-Akbari*, vol. II, p. 180
4 Fitch, in Hakluyt, vol. v, p. 474
5 Monserrate, p. 12
6 Fitch, in Hakluyt, vol. v, p. 474
7 ibid.
8 Monserrate, p. 36
9 ibid.
10 Abul Fazl vol. I, p. 222
11 Monserrate, pp. 200–01
12 ibid. p. 201
13 ibid. p. 200
14 ibid. p. 88
15 Bartoli, p. 14
16 ibid. p. 15
17 Monserrate, p. 43
18 Fitch, in Hakluyt, vol. v, p. 474
19 Monserrate, p. 64
20 ibid. p. 176
21 ibid. p. 79
22 Fitch, in Hakluyt, vol. v, p. 475
23 ibid.
24 ibid.

VI A rich and prosperous country

1 Fitch, in Hakluyt, vol. v, p. 475
2 ibid.
3 ibid.
4 ibid.
5 ibid.
6 ibid.
7 ibid. p. 476
8 ibid.
9 ibid.
10 ibid.
11 ibid.
12 ibid.
13 ibid.
14 ibid.
15 ibid.
16 ibid. p. 478
17 ibid. p. 477
18 ibid.
19 ibid. p. 478
20 ibid.
21 ibid. p. 477
22 ibid.
23 ibid.
24 ibid.

25 ibid.
26 ibid. p. 478
27 ibid. p. 480
28 ibid. p. 478
29 ibid.
30 ibid. p. 479
31 ibid.
32 ibid. pp. 479–80
33 ibid. p. 476
34 Bernier, p. 334
35 Fitch, in Hakluyt, vol. v, p. 480
36 ibid.
37 ibid.
38 ibid.
39 ibid. p. 481
40 ibid. p. 480
41 ibid. p. 481
42 ibid.
43 Monserrate, p. 25
44 Fitch, in Hakluyt, vol. v, p. 481
45 ibid.
46 ibid.
47 ibid. p. 482
48 ibid.
49 ibid. p. 483
50 ibid.
51 ibid.
52 ibid. p. 484
53 ibid.
54 ibid.
55 Monserrate, p. 106
56 Fitch, in Hakluyt, vol. v, p. 482
57 ibid. p. 483
58 Frederick (Federici), in Purchas, vol. X, p. 113
59 ibid. pp. 113–14
60 ibid. p. 114
61 Fitch, in Hakluyt, vol. v, p. 482
62 Manrique, vol. I, p. 198
63 Bernier, p. 175
64 Shiab-ud-din Talish, pp. 420–21
65 Bernier, pp. 175–76
66 Fitch, in Hakluyt, vol. v, p. 484
67 ibid.
68 ibid.
69 ibid.
70 ibid. p. 485

VII Lord of the White Elephant

1 Fitch, in Hakluyt, vol. v, p. 485
2 ibid.
3 Balbi, in Purchas, vol. X, p. 150
4 ibid.
5 Fitch, in Hakluyt, vol. v, p. 485
6 ibid.
7 ibid.
8 Balbi, in Purchas, vol. X p. 151
9 Fitch, in Hakluyt, vol. v, p. 486
10 Balbi, in Purchas, vol. X, p. 153
11 Fitch, in Hakluyt, vol. v, p. 486
12 ibid. p. 488
13 ibid.
14 ibid. p. 489
15 ibid.
16 ibid.
17 ibid. p. 487
18 ibid. p. 491
19 ibid.
20 ibid.
21 ibid. p. 492
22 Frederick (Federici), in Purchas, vol. X, p. 130
23 Fitch, in Hakluyt, vol. v, p. 487
24 ibid.
25 ibid.
26 ibid.
27 ibid.
28 ibid.
29 ibid. p. 488
30 ibid.
31 Manrique, vol. II, p. 197
32 Fitch, in Hakluyt, vol. v, p. 487

33 Frederick (Federici) in Purchas, vol. X, p. 127
34 ibid.
35 Fitch, in Hakluyt, vol. v, p. 491
36 Balbi, in Purchas, vol. X, p. 157
37 ibid. p. 158
38 ibid.
39 ibid.
40 ibid. p. 159
41 ibid. p. 160
42 ibid.
43 ibid.
44 ibid.
45 ibid. p. 161
46 ibid.
47 Fitch, in Hakluyt, vol. v, p. 490
48 ibid.
49 ibid.
50 ibid.
51 ibid.
52 *Hmannan Yazawin*, vol. III, p. 34
53 Fitch, in Hakluyt, vol. v, p. 491
54 Balbi, in Purchas, vol. X, p. 154
55 Fitch, in Hakluyt, vol. v, p. 493
56 ibid.
57 ibid.
58 ibid.
59 Balbi, in Purchas, vol. X, p. 155
60 Fitch, in Hakluyt, vol. v, p. 493
61 ibid. p. 494
62 ibid.
63 ibid. p. 490
64 ibid. p. 495
65 ibid.
66 ibid.
67 ibid.
68 ibid.
69 ibid.
70 ibid. p. 496
71 ibid.
72 ibid. p. 497
73 ibid.
74 ibid.
75 ibid. p. 496
76 ibid. p. 497

VIII Gateway to Cathay

1 Fitch, in Hakluyt, vol. v, p. 497
2 ibid. pp. 497—98
3 Frederick (Federici), in Purchas, vol. X, p. 115
4 ibid. p. 116
5 ibid.
6 ibid.
7 Barbosa, vol. I, p. 200f.
8 ibid.
9 d'Eredia, p. 19
10 Fitch, in Hakluyt, vol. v, p. 498
11 Pinto, vol. II, p. 300ff.
12 d'Eredia p. 20
13 Fitch, in Hakluyt, vol. v, p. 498
14 ibid.
15 ibid.
16 ibid. p. 499
17 ibid.
18 ibid.
19 ibid.
20 ibid.
21 ibid.
22 ibid.
23 ibid.
24 ibid. p. 500

IX The journey home

1 Fitch, in Hakluyt, vol. v, p. 500
2 ibid.
3 ibid.
4 ibid.
5 ibid.
6 ibid. pp. 500–01
7 Barros and Couto vol. X, p. 151

8 Fitch, in Hakluyt, vol. v, p. 501
9 ibid.
10 ibid.
11 ibid.
12 ibid.
13 ibid.
14 ibid. p. 500
15 ibid. p.501
16 Rebeiro pp. 74–77
17 Fitch, in Hakluyt, vol. v, p. 501
18 Da Gama, vol. I, p. 331
19 Fitch, in Hakluyt, vol. v, p. 503
20 ibid. p. 502
21 ibid.
22 ibid.
23 Frederick (Federici), in Purchas, vol. X, p. 104
24 Fitch, in Hakluyt, vol. v, pp. 502–03
25 Da Orta, p. 141
26 Fitch, in Hakluyt, vol. v, p. 505
27 ibid.
28 ibid.
29 ibid.

X Charter for empire

1 Fitch, in Hakluyt, vol. v, p. 503
2 ibid.
3 ibid. p. 504
4 ibid.
5 ibid.
6 ibid.
7 ibid.
8 ibid.
9 Carletti, p. 195
10 Hakluyt, vol. VI, p. 73
11 British Museum Lansdowne MSS, No. 241, fol. 395b (modernised spelling)
12 ibid. fol. 51b
13 Stevens and Birdwood, p. 1
14 ibid. p. 5
15 Beveridge, vol. I, p. 227
16 Stevens and Birdwood, p. 26
17 ibid. pp. 36–37
18 Birdwood, pp. 163–89
19 ibid. p. 123
20 ibid. p. 103

Index

ABDULLAH KHAN, 61
ABRAHAM, 154
ABUL FAZL, 66
Acheh and the Achinese, 131–3, 166
Aden, 167–8
ADHAM KHAN, 59–60
Agra, 53, 56, 61–6, 68, 78, 89
AKBAR, emperor (Zelabdim Echebar, the Great Mogor), 7, 18–19, 30, 47, 53, 56–63, 65–79, 85–6, 89, 94–5, 156
ALAUNGSITHU, 118
ALBUQUERQUE, Alfonso d', 127–8
Aleppo, 18, 23, 25–8, 77, 154–5, 159, 160
Allahabad, 78–80
Amangao, *see* Macao
ANAWRAHAHTA, 118
ANTONIO, Don, 16, 27, 29, 31, 43
Antwerp, 17
AQUAVIVA, Father, 57, 70–2
Arakan and the Arakanese, 92–4, 100–2, 107, 142
Ava, 110–11
Ayuthia, 102, 108

BABA KAPUR, 86
Babel, Tower of, 25
BABUR, emperor, 47
Baghdad, 18–19, 24–5, 154
BAHADUR SHAH, sultan of Cambay, 30
Bahrein, 27, 146
BALBI, Gaspar, 96–7, 109–12, 119
Banaras, 81, 84
Banda, 157
Bantam, 166–7
BARBOSA, Duarte, 127
Barisal, 94
Basra, 19, 23, 25–6, 28, 153–4
Bassein, 30, 97, 136, 142
BAYIN-NAUNG, 100, 102, 109, 112–18, 122
BAZ BAHADUR, of Malwa, 59–60
Belgaum, 46
Bengal, 77, 86, 88–9, 92–5, 108, 130, 142
Bhutan, 87
Bidar, 53, 56
Bijapur, 44, 46, 47–9
Bima, 140
Birejik, 24, 154
Borneo, 130, 140, 157
Botanter, *see* Bhutan
'Bread, King of', *see* MIRZA ALI
BURGHLEY, Lord, 157, 159
Burhanpur, 56, 58
Bushire, 26

CAEIRO, Joao, 100–1
Calicut, 148–51
Cambay, 30, 57, 168
Cambodia, 130, 158
Cannanore, 151
Canton, 137, 139
CARLETTI, Francesco, 124
CAROM, Isabel de, 39
CARVALHO, Alberto, 95–7, 104
CAVENDISH, Thomas, 134

Ceylon, 52, 113, 118
Chaliyam, 150
Chaul, 31, 49, 153
Chiengmai, 111, 121–2, 124
China, emperor of, 19
Chittagong, 90–4, 96
Christian Purana, 32
Cochin, 126–9, 130, 136, 142, 146–51, 153
Cochin China, 158
Colombo, 116–17, 143–5
Comorin, Cape, 146
Constantinople, 15–16, 26, 77, 154, 159–60
Cooch Behar, 86–8
Coromandel, 103, 130
Cosmin, 97
'Cutup de Lashash', *see* MUHAMMAD KULI KUTB SHAH

Daman, 30, 136
Deccan, 50
Dianga, 93
Diu, 26, 30
DRAKE, Sir Francis, 17, 29
Dutch, the, 160–1, 166

East India Company, English, 8, 165–9
Edward Bonaventure, 160
ELDRED, John, 18, 24–6, 161–2
ELIZABETH I, queen, 15–16, 19, 29, 125, 161–2, 164–6
Estavam, Father, *see* STEVENS

Fatehpur Sikri, 62, 64–5, 67–70, 72–3, 76–8, 95
FEDERICI, Cesar, 8, 90–2, 125–6, 151
Fellujah, 24
FITCH, Ralph, 8–9, 18–20, 29–30, 169
  leaves England, 21
  in the Near East, 21–6, 28
  journey to Goa, 29–31
  in Goa, 32–3, 36, 39–41, 43–45
  journey to Agra, 46–58, 60–1
  in Agra, 62–4
  in Fatehpur Sikri, 69–74, 76–8
  journey through northern India, 78–91
  in Arakan, 91–4
  in Bengal again, 94–5
  journey to Burma, 96–7
  in Burma, 98–109, 112, 118–25
  journey to Malacca, 125–6
  in Malacca, 126, 129–31, 134, 136–41
  journey home, 142–8, 150–6
  in London, 156–9
  returns to Levant, 159–60
  in London again, 160–4, 166–8
  death, 168
Fugger, banking house, 134
Fukien, 138

GAMA, Vasco da, 36, 143, 148–9
GARRETT, William, 15
Goa, 26–47, 49, 57, 61, 69, 72, 88–9, 94, 113–15, 130, 133, 136, 138, 140, 142, 144–5, 150, 153
Golconda, 49–53
Great Susan, 15
Gujarat, 30, 167
Gwalior, 86

Hainan, 158
HAKLUYT, Richard, 7–8, 157, 160
HARBORNE, William, 15–16, 26
Hawai, elephant, 75–6
HAWKINS, William, 168
'Hell, mouth of', 25
Hijli, 90–1
Hmawdin pagoda, 96

HOSHANG SHAH, of Mandu, 59
Hugli, 88, 90, 93, 134, 140

Indies, Portuguese viceroy of the, 36–7, 40, 42–5, 69, 88, 93, 113–15
Inquisition, the, 30–31, 41–3, 115, 149
ISA KHAN, 95

Jafna, 113–16
JAHANGIR, emperor, 63, 65, 168
Jambi (or Jamba), 140–1
JAMES I, king, 167–9
Java and the Javanese, 128–30, 140, 158, 166–7
Johore, 131, 133
Johore Lama, 133

Kalanaur, 88
Kandy, 113–15, 117–18, 144–5
Kotte, 143–4
KUNJALI MARAKKA, 150
Kurdistan, 154
Kyushu, 138

Laban, 140
Labuan, 140
Lahore, 77, 157
LANCASTER, James, 160, 162, 166
LEEDES, William, 18, 26, 32–3, 40, 43, 46, 60, 62, 77
Levant Company, 15, 21, 23, 156–7, 159–61
LINSCHOTEN, Jan van, 32–6, 44
Lisbon, 17, 33, 40, 43, 45, 149

Macao, 125, 134–5, 137–8
Macassar, 130
Madras, 103
MAGELLAN, Ferdinand, 127
MAHMUD BEGARHA, sultan of Cambay, 30
Makhau, 100
Malabar, 93, 148–9, 151–3, 157
Malacca, 18, 39, 89–90, 93–4, 125–7, 129–34, 136–8, 140–2, 166
Malwa, 59–60
Mandu, 58–9
Mardin, 154
Martaban, 100–1, 103, 125, 142
Masulipatam, 52–3
Mergui, 125
MIRZA ALI, sultan of Bidar, 53
Mocha, 52
Mogul, the Great, *see* AKBAR
Mokeik, 121
Moluccas, the, 29, 157
MONSERRATE, Father, 57–8, 60–1, 70, 72–3, 75, 86, 88
Mosul, 154
MUHAMMAD HAKIM, 73–4
MUHAMMAD KULI KUTB SHAH, of Golconda, 50–1
MURAD, prince, 70

Nagasaki, 138
NANDA-BAYIN, 109–12, 121–2
Negrais, 96–7, 102
NEWBERY, John, 19–21, 23, 25–9, 32–3, 40, 43, 46, 56, 60, 62, 73–4, 76–7, 95, 125, 142, 156–7

Orissa, 94
Ormuz, 18, 26–9, 32, 153–4
ORTA, Garcia da, 152
OSBORNE, Sir Edward, 15–16, 18, 159

Patna, 84–6
Pegu, 53, 77, 97–8, 100, 102–3, 106, 108–9, 117–19, 121, 124–5, 132, 134, 142, 146
Peking, 139
PHILIP II, king of Spain, 16, 27, 44–5, 61, 70, 88, 110, 162

Philippines, the, 130
Pipli, 94
PLANTIN, Christopher, 70
POLO, Marco, 49
Porto Grande, *see* Chittagong
Porto Piqueno, *see* Satgaon
Portugal and the Portuguese, 16–18, 26–7, 29–31, 34–5, 37–42, 45–6, 69–70, 72, 88–90, 92–5, 100–2, 108–10, 113–15, 119–120, 125–37, 139–40, 142–43, 145, 148–54, 160, 162, 164, 166, 168
Povoacao do Nome de Deos na China, *see* Macao
Prayag, *see* Allahabad
Prome, 100, 111
Punjab, 78, 88
PURCHAS, Samuel, 157

Quilon, 147, 151

RAJASINHA, 144–5
Rajputana, 78
ROE, Sir Thomas, 168
RUPMATI, 59–60

Saint George's Island, 21
SALIM CHISTI, 65
Salsette island, 31
Sambhur, lake, 78
Sandwip, 96
SANTA FE, Antonio de, 38
San Thome, 103
Satgaon, 90–1
Saugur, 91
SEIXAS, Paolo da, 101
Servidore, *see* Shehrbidar
SHAH JAHAN, emperor, 59
Shans, the, 100, 122
Shehrbidar, 53
Siam and the Siamese, 101–2, 108, 130, 137, 158
Sikri, 65–6
SIQUEIRA, Diego Lopez de, 126–7
Sironj, 60
Sitawaka, 144
SMITH, Thomas, 15
Socotra, 27, 167
Solor, 93
Sonargaon, 95
Spain and the Spaniards, 16–17, 153, 156, 162, 164, 167
Sripur, 95
STAPER, Richard, 15–16, 18
STEVENS, Father Thomas, 32–3, 44
STORY, James, 18, 26, 32–3, 44–5, 72
STROPENE, Michael, 27, 29
Surat, 130, 168
Syriam, 103

TABIN SHWE-TI, 100–2, 112, 118
TABORER, Andreas, 43–4
Taj Mahal, 59
Talaings, the, 100–1, 110
Tanda, 86
TAVARES, Pedro, 89–90
Tavoy, 101, 125
Tenasserim, 125–6, 142
Thana, 31
THARRAWADY-MIN, 122
Timor, 93, 157
Tipperah, 91–2
Toungoo, 100, 111
Tripoli (Lebanon), 21, 23, 154–5
Turkey and the Turks, 15, 26, 159
Tyger, 7, 21, 23

Ujjain, 60

Vijayanagar, 47, 53

XAVIER, St Francis, 37–9, 113, 131–2

Zelabdim Echebar, *see* AKBAR